MICROSOFT WORD

MICROSOFT WORD MADE SIMPLE FOR BEGINNERS:

A Beginners Guide to Microsoft Word

BONIFACE BENEDICT

MICROSOFT WORD

DEDICATION

This book is dedicated to all computer lovers all over the world.

COPYRIGHT

Do not use any part of this book in any form – electronic, mechanical or physical without an express written permission from the author.

In case of any reference to any content in this book you should make adequate reference.

MICROSOFT WORD

TABLE OF CONTENTS

DEDICATION ii
COPYRIGHT iii
INTRODUCTION 1
CHAPTER 1 4
WELCOME TO WORD 4
    The Unimaginative Way To Start Word 6
    How to open a blank Microsoft page 8
    RIBBONS 9
    WORKING IN THE WORD ENVIRONMENT 9
    Customize the Ribbon 14
    SHOWING AND HIDING THE RIBBON 15
    Using the Tell me feature 17
    The Quick Access Toolbar 17
    The Ruler 19
    Backstage view 20
    Document views and zooming 20
    Ribbon tab shortcuts 24
    Closing a Document 24
CHAPTER 2 26

FONT FUN 26
- Describing text 27
- Understanding text attributes 30
- Selecting the proper typeface 34
- Font Control 35
- Font Specifications and Standards 36
- Using the Font dialog box 38
- Choosing fonts with a theme 40
- Changing the Default Font 41
- Typography Control 43
- Changing text scale 43
- Setting character spacing 45
- Adding kerning and ligatures 46
- Adjusting text position 49
- Accessing the Format Text Effects pane 52
- Changing text fill 53
- Setting a text outline 55
- Creating hidden Text 57
- Find and Replace Text Formatting 60

CHAPTER 3 66
PAGE FORMATTING 66
- Page Formatting 67
- Types of Documents 67
- Page Setup 68

Margins, Header, and Footer 71
Accessing the Header and Footer Page Areas 73
Change Page Margin Size 75
Formatting E-books 76
Changing the Document Layout 77
Header and Footer for Normal Documents 79
Formatting PDF Files 84
Formatting Booklets 87
Conclusion 97
CHAPTER 4 98
TEXT EDITION 98
Edit a Microsoft Word document 99
Selecting Partial Words 101
Controlling Paste Formatting 104
CHAPTER 5 107
AUTOCORRECT, AUTOTEXT, AND AUTOFORMAT 107
Know Your Autos 107
Working with AutoCorrect capitalization settings 109
Undoing an AutoCorrect change 114
Understanding AutoFormat options 115
CHAPTER 6 119
FORMATING TABLES 119
Inserting Tables 119
Typing Text in Table Cells 121

Convert Table to Text and Vice Versa 123

Selecting and Deleting Tables and Cells 128

Selecting All Table Cells to Delete a Table 130

Selecting a Single Cell 131

Selecting Table Rows and Columns 132

Inserting Table Rows, Columns, and Cells.......................... 133

Using Table ➤ Insert Command 134

Merging Cells... 136

Changing Cell, Column, or Row Dimensions 138

Deleting Table Cells, Rows, and Columns 138

Table Alignment and Position 140

Changing Table Row Size 143

Changing Table Column Size 145

Changing Cell Dimensions and Vertical Alignment 147

Auto-Generate Table of Content.. 148

CHAPTER 7 150

CREATING AND USING TEMPLATES 150

What Is a Template? 150

Types of Word Templates... 152

Templates with Formatting and Controls 154

How to personalize Microsoft template for yourself 155

Save a template 156

CHAPTER 8 158

MICROSOFT WORD

COMMON MICROSOFT WORD PROBLEMS AND POSSIBLE SOLUTIONS 158
   Launch Word in Safe Mode & Disable Add-Ins 158
   Problem related to editing a document 161
   What to Do When You Can't Edit Word Document.............. 162
   TEN FUNCTION KEY 167
      Shortcuts... 167

INTRODUCTION

This book goes way beyond the beginner's user-level when it comes to word processing with Microsoft Word. This isn't a technical book, but rather a book geared toward the professional or anyone else who is serious about the words they write.

Word is a powerful program, and few people venture into its more sophisticated capacities. That's sad because many of Word's features can save you time and help you create a better document.

It is a pleasure to write this guide on using MS Word for you. So here is the result, and I genuinely hope that you like it or, even better, that you learn from it.

Although it offers extreme simplicity in its usage, Word also has in-depth typographical knowledge and rules so that anyone can perform adequately with it. While Word is easy to use, it is often misunderstood because it is so rich in typographic tools.

And it is due to it being so enterprising in its aim to be a printing-style tool that is easy to use with a powerful effect. The Word can sometimes become hard to comprehend as it is hard not to get mad about a Word document that:

• Refuses to obey the formatting options that need to be applied?
• Seems not effective in formatting text into a table?
• Cannot hold title headers and other items (such as figures) as the document is being edited?
• Refuses to perform many other "simple" things we want to do or have difficulty in execution?

What's in the book?

Are you still reading the introduction? That's weird. Most people don't even bother, since you do, I'm pleased.

Each chapter covers a topic and significant sections within the chapter go into detail. At the end, I indeed expect that you will suddenly have that intense feeling of final mastery.

Screenshots are from Windows 10 and Word 2016 versions. You may see small differences from the ones you see on your computer but much of this book can be used with earlier versions of Word.

Multiple key combinations are also presented:
Ctrl+Shift+S

Here you press Ctrl and Shift together and then tap the S key and it will release all the keys.

Word presents its commands on a Ribbon. The commands are organized into tabs and then groups.

Each command is a button, and the button's artwork appears in this book's margins.

Some buttons feature menus; to view the menu, you either click the button or click a down-pointing triangle next to the button. The text directs you on whether to click the button or its menu.

When a menu features a submenu, this text uses the following format to show how the submenu or command is chosen:

Page Number ⇨ Current Position ⇨ Plain Number

This direction tells you to click the Page Number button and, from its menu, choose the Current Position submenu and then the Plain Number item.

More specific directions for some of the unusual things Word does are explained throughout the text.

Your Feedback Is Very Important

MICROSOFT WORD

Before you continue reading, I would like to say that your opinion is critical to me. I don't know how many of you will write to me to give any comment, but I hope to answer everyone and, whenever it's possible, resolve questions or problems that arise.

Since I have many other duties, sometimes it may take a little while before I can answer you, but I promise to do my best. Please feel free to write me at the following e-mail address:

CHAPTER 1

WELCOME TO WORD

This book does intend to teach you how to use Microsoft Word. It assumes that you are new th the software, plus if you already have some knowledge about: how to open, change, and save documents, and how you can format text. Follow up again to learn a new idea.

This very brief chapter is just a primer about Microsoft Word, so you can easily have the feeling of mastery when people around you talk about Microsoft word.

MICROSOFT WORD

Opening Word

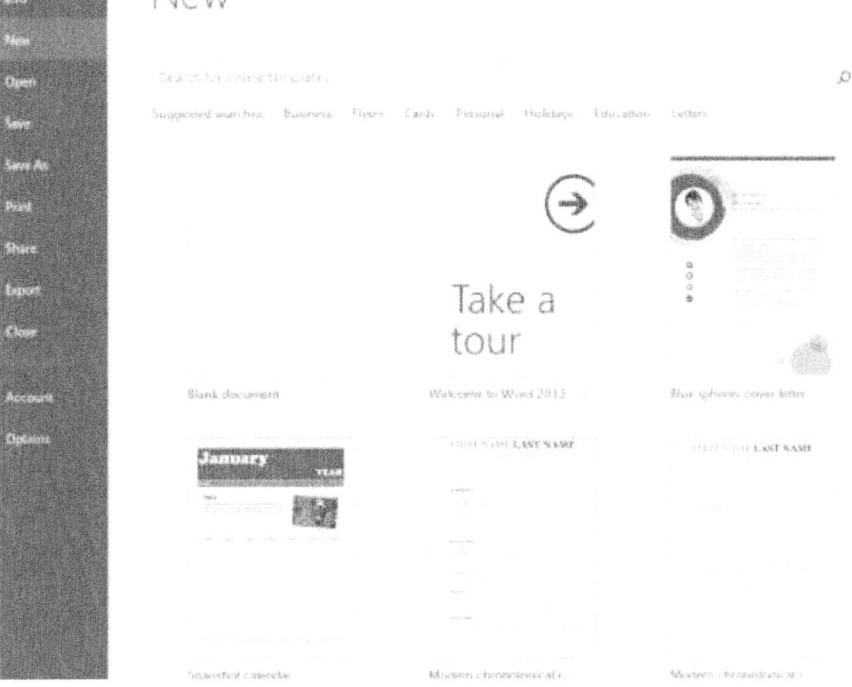

Microsoft Word New Template selection page

MICROSOFT WORD

The Unimaginative Way To Start Word

You can start Word in several ways, then create documents to your preference. But before you can start Word, your computer must be **ON** and adequately moderate. After you log into Windows, you can get Word going wthout delay, the place to start any program in Windows is at the fabled Start button. It may not be the fastest or the most exciting or convenient way to start a program, but it's consistent and reliable:

Click the Start button (which is decorated with the Windows logo).

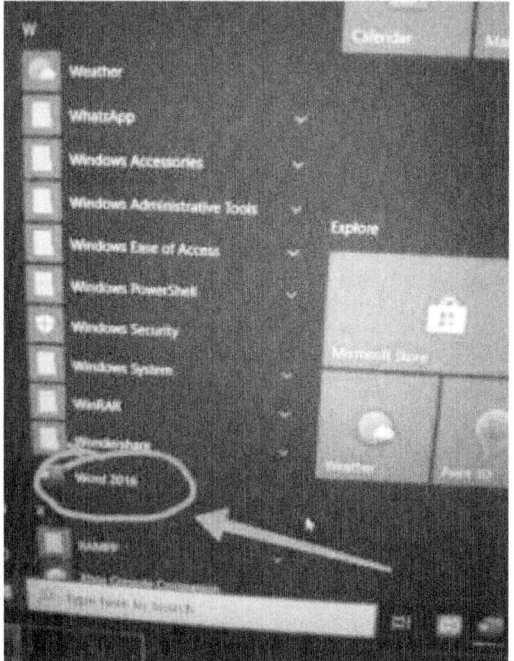

Figure 1.1 showing all programs on a PC

MICROSOFT WORD

Now, the Start menu appears. You might find the Microsoft Word program icon right there on the Start menu. If you see the Word icon, click it to run the program.

Or also, choose All Programs to pop up the All Programs menu, and then select Microsoft Word. (Shown in figure 1.1 above).

Alternatively, you can also choose the Microsoft Office item (submenu) to display its contents, and then select Microsoft Word.

Note: If you can't find Word anywhere on the All Programs menu, it may not be installed on your computer.

The Better Way To Start Word

When you use Word a lot, it is required to have quick access to its program icon by creating a Word shortcut icon on your desktop, to do this:

- Locate the **Word icon** on the **Start button's All Programs menu.**
- Don't click to start Word now!
- **Right-click** the **Microsoft Word menu** item.
- A pop-up menu appears
- Choose **to Send Desktop** (Create Shortcut).
- Press the Esc key to hide the Start button menu and view the desktop.

You haven't changed anything, but you have added the Word program icon to the desktop. You can use that icon to start Word, so double-click the icon, and Word starts.

Another way to have the Word icon always handy is to pin it to the Start menu directly. In Step 3, choose the item named Pin to Start

Menu. That way, the Word icon always appear at the top of the list on the Start button menu.

How to open a blank Microsoft page

Opening a Word document causes Word to start and to display a document for editing, printing, or just giving others the impression that you're doing something. Locate the Word document icon in a folder window and double-click to open that document.

In Windows 10, you can see a Jump List of recently opened documents by either right-clicking the Word icon on the taskbar or clicking the right-pointing arrow next to the Word icon on the Start button menu. Select a document from the list to start Word and open that document.

RIBBONS

WORKING IN THE WORD ENVIRONMENT

> A ribbon may refer to any of the following:
>
> 1. When referring to impact printing, a ribbon is a device used to transfer ink to paper. Ribbons are mostly seen on devices such as typewriters and stenotype machines.
>
> 2. When referring to Microsoft Office programs such as Microsoft Word and Excel, the Ribbon is a feature that replaces the traditional file menu. As shown in the image, the Ribbon dynamically changes based on what the user is currently doing. In this example, the Ribbon for "Write" is being displayed.

The Ribbon is the crucial way you work in Microsoft Office. Depending on what you're trying to do, the Ribbon will change to offer all the accessible commands for your current task or screen. But you're not stuck with the Ribbon as it is. You can customize it, keep following through this teaching, so you can have 100% control of the Ribbon. You can add and remove groups and individual icons to and from the Ribbon. You can rearrange the icons in the Ribbon. You can also export your Ribbon customizations and import them to Office on another computer.

MICROSOFT WORD

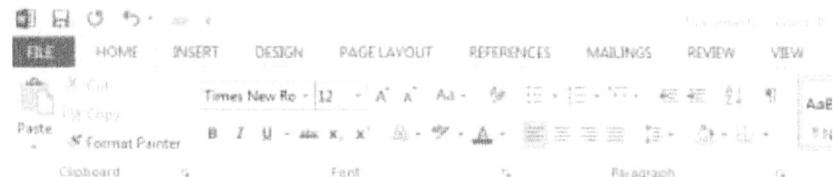

Figure 1.3 Ribbon in

First, let's cover how the Ribbon works. Each Office application offers different sets of Ribbons depending on what you're trying to do. A **Home Ribbon** offers general commands and features, a **View Ribbon** provides icons for changing the view of your screen or document, and an **Insert Ribbon** includes icons for inserting different objects and items. Each Ribbon contains a unique set of groups and commands for specific functions. **Ribbons** are also **known as tabs** since you click on the tab at the top of the screen to display a certain Ribbon.

Each Ribbon is arranged into sections known as groups to organize similar icons. One group may contain icons devoted to fonts, a second group with icons devoted to page setup, the third group with icons for styles, and the fourth group with icons for themes. When you customize your Ribbons, you typically want to keep icons with similar functions in the same group.

Knowing the Ribbon is important.

The Home tab:

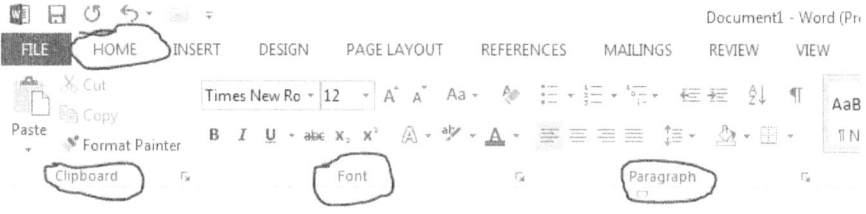

MICROSOFT WORD

The Home tab is the default tab in Microsoft Word. It has five groups of related commands; Clipboard, Font, Paragraph, Styles and Editing. It helps you change document settings like font size, adding bullets, adjusting styles and many other common features. It also helps you to return to the home section of the document.

The Insert tab:

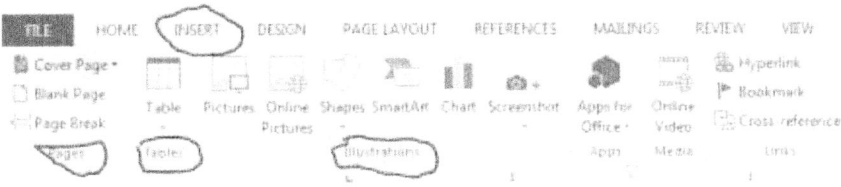

Insert Tab is the second tab in the Ribbon. As the name suggests, it is used to insert or add extra features in your document. It is commonly used to add tables, pictures, clip art, shapes, page number, etc. The Insert tab has seven groups of related commands; Pages, Tables, Illustrations, Links, Header & Footer, Text and Symbols.

Page Layout tab:

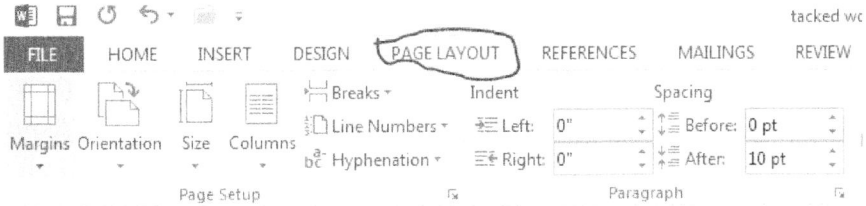

MICROSOFT WORD

Design tab

It is the fourth tab in the Ribbon. This tab allows you to control the look and feel of your document, i.e. you can change the page size, margins, line spacing, indentation, documentation orientation, etc. The Page Layout tab has five groups of related commands; Themes, Page Setup, Page Background, Paragraph and Arrange.

The References tab:

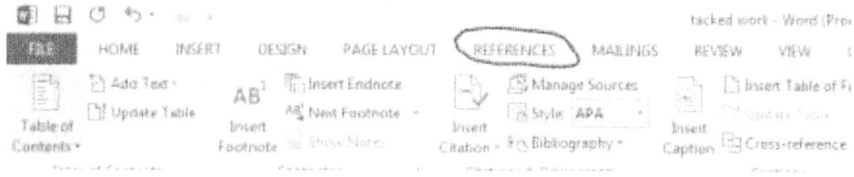

It is the fifth tab in the Ribbon. It allows you to enter document sources, citations, bibliography commands, etc. It also offers commands to create a table of contents, an index, table of contents and table of authorities. The References tab has six groups of related commands; Table of Contents, Footnotes, Citations & Bibliography, Captions, Index and Table of Authorities

The Mailings tab:

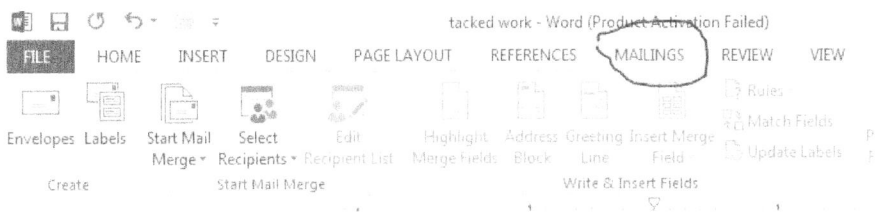

It is the sixth tab in the ribbon. It is the least-often used tab of all the tabs available in the Ribbon. It allows you merge emails, writing and inserting different fields, preview results and convert a file into a PDF format. The Mailings tab has five groups of related commands; Create, Start Mail Merge, Write & Insert Fields, Preview Results and Finish.

The Review tab:

It is the seventh tab in the Ribbon. This tab offers you some important commands to modify your document. It helps you proofread your content, to add or remove comments, track changes, etc. The Review tab has six groups of related commands; Proofing, Comments, Tracking, Changes, Compare and Protect.

MICROSOFT WORD

The View tab:

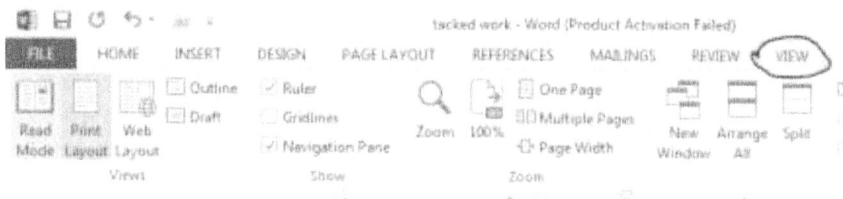

The View tab is located next to the Review tab. This tab allows you to switch between Single Page and Two Page views. It also enables you to control various layout tools like boundaries, guides, rulers. Its primary purpose is to offer you different ways to view your document. The View tab has five groups of related commands; Document Views, Show/Hide, Zoom, Window and Macros

Customize the Ribbon

Add or remove tabs from the Ribbon and add or remove items on those tabs by customizing the Ribbon to meet your needs. As a precaution, don't make too many changes until you are familiar with how the Ribbon is set up by default.

MICROSOFT WORD

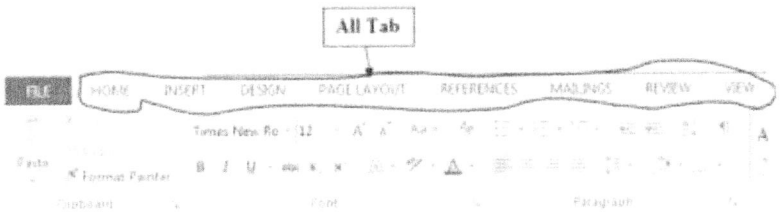

What you can't customize: You can't reduce the size of your ribbon, or the size of the text or the icons on the ribbon. The only way to do this is to change your display resolution, which would change the size of everything on your page.

When you customize your ribbon: Your customizations only apply to the Office program you're working in at the time. For example, if you personalize your ribbon in PowerPoint, those same changes won't be visible in Excel. If you want similar customizations in your other Office apps, you'll have to open each of those apps to make the same changes.

SHOWING AND HIDING THE RIBBON

If you find that the Ribbon takes up too much screen space, you can hide it. To do this, **click the Ribbon Display Options arrow** in the upper-right corner of the Ribbon, then **select the desired option from the drop-down menu**:

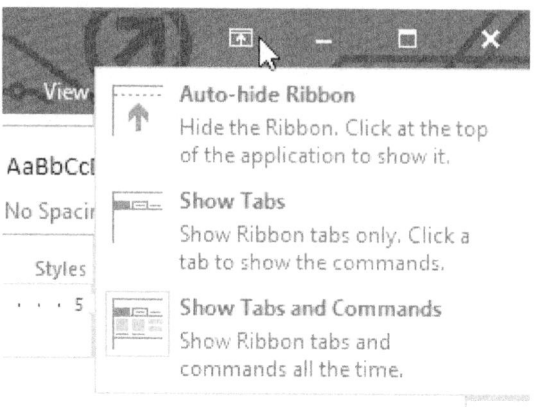

- Auto-hide Ribbon: Auto-hide displays your document in full-screen mode and completely hides the Ribbon from view. To show the Ribbon, **click the Expand Ribbon command** at the top of screen.

- Show Tabs: This option hides all command groups when they're not in use, but tabs will remain visible. To **show the Ribbon, simply click a tab**.

- Show Tabs and Commands: This option maximizes the Ribbon. All of the tabs and commands will be visible. This option is selected by default when you open Word for the first time.

• *To learn how to add custom tabs and commands to the Ribbon, review our Extra on Customizing the Ribbon.*

MICROSOFT WORD

Using the Tell me feature

If you're having trouble finding the command you want, the Tell Me feature can help. It works just like a regular search bar: Type what you're looking for, and a list of options will appear. You can then use the command directly from the menu without having to find it on the Ribbon.

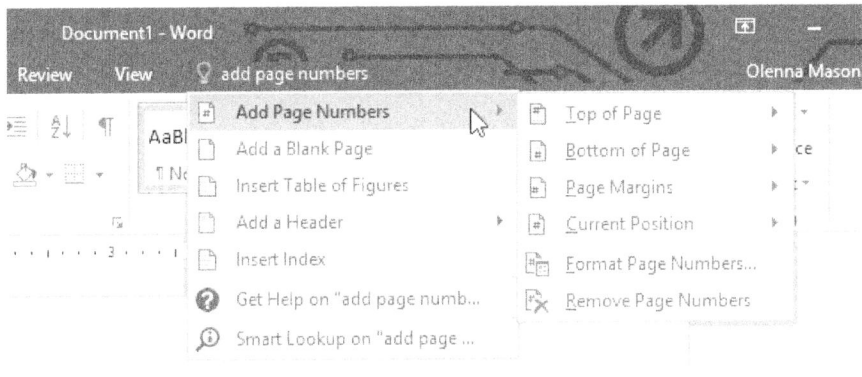

The Quick Access Toolbar

Located just above the Ribbon, the Quick Access Toolbar lets you access common commands no matter which tab is selected. By default, it shows the Save, Undo, and Redo commands, but you can add other commands depending on your needs.

To add commands to the Quick Access Toolbar:

1. Click the drop-down arrow to the right of the Quick Access Toolbar.

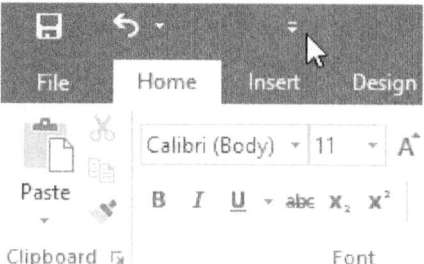

2. Select the command you want to add from the menu.

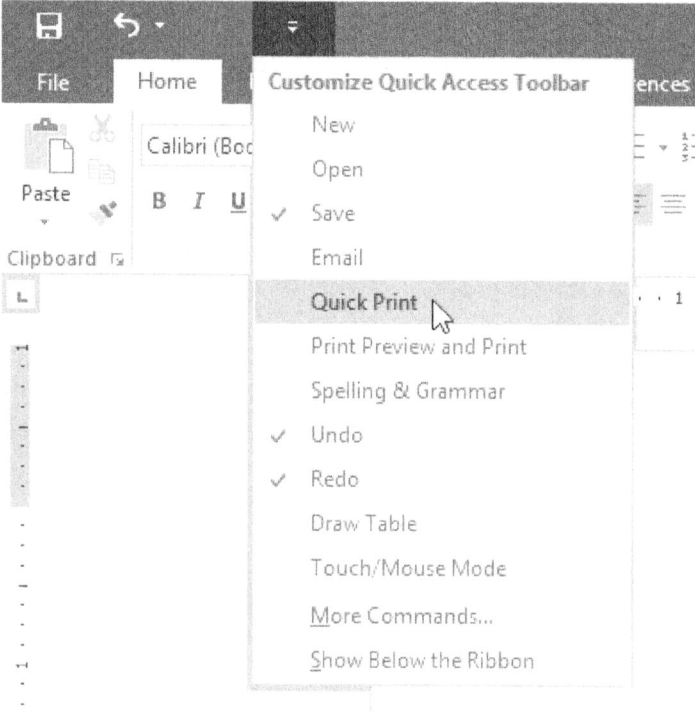

3. The command will be added to the Quick Access Toolbar.

MICROSOFT WORD

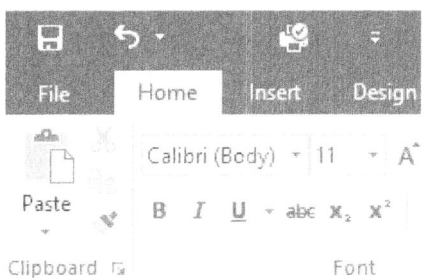

The Ruler

The Ruler is located at the top and to the left of your document. It makes it easier to adjust your document with precision. If you want, you can hide the Ruler to create more screen space.

To show or hide the Ruler:

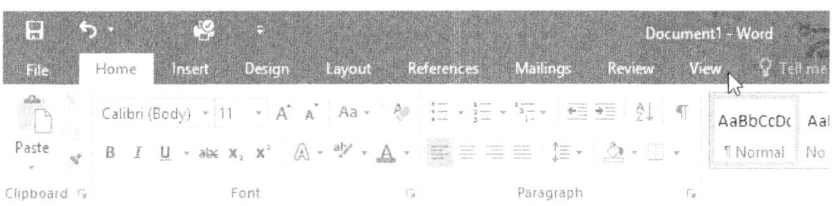

- Click the View tab.

- Now, click on the checkbox next to Ruler to show or hide the Ruler.

MICROSOFT WORD

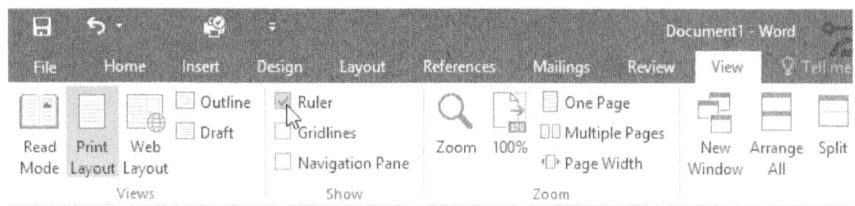

Backstage view

Backstage view gives you various options for saving, opening a file, printing, and sharing your document. To access Backstage view, click the File tab on the Ribbon.

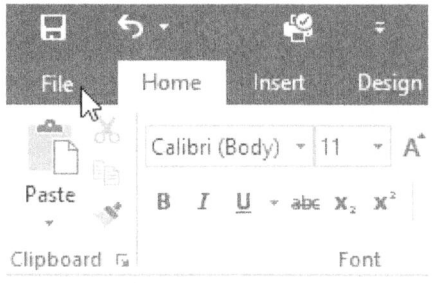

Document views and zooming

Word has a variety of viewing options that change how your document is displayed. You can choose to view your document in **Read Mode, Print Layout, or Web Layout.** These views can be useful for various tasks, especially if you're planning to print the document. You can also zoom in and out to make your document easier to read.

Switching document views

Switching between different document views is easy. Just locate and select the desired document view command in the bottom-right corner of the Word window.

- Read Mode: This view opens the document to a full screen. This view is great for reading large amounts of text or simply reviewing your work.

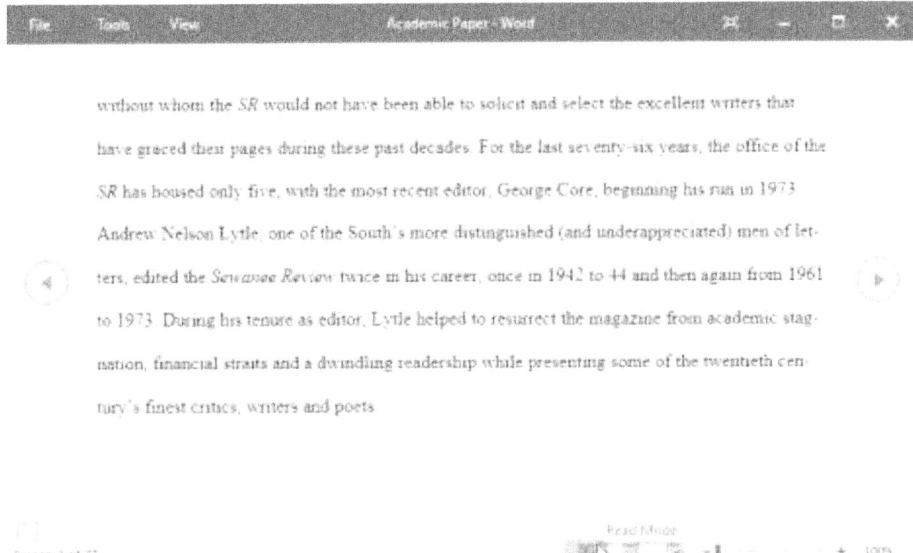

- Print Layout: This is the default document view in Word. It shows what the document will look like on the printed page.

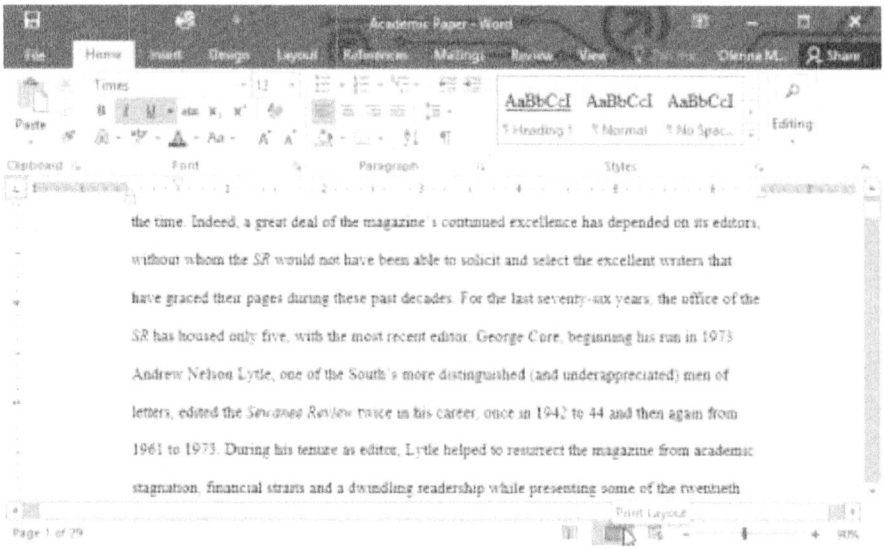

- Web Layout: This view displays the document as a webpage, which can be helpful if you're using Word to publish content online.

MICROSOFT WORD

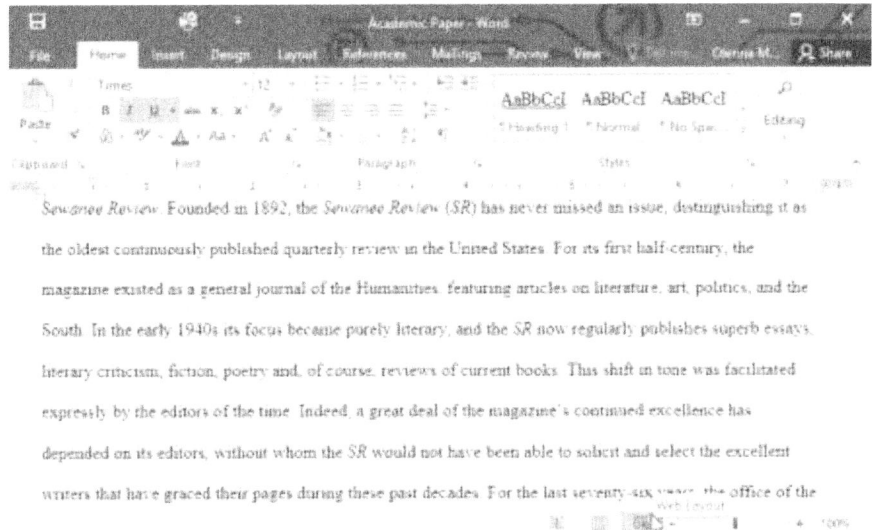

Zooming in and out

To zoom in or out, click and drag the zoom control slider in the bottom-right corner of the Word window. You can also select the **+ or - commands** to zoom in or out by smaller increments. The number next to the slider displays the current zoom percentage, also called the zoom level.

Ribbon tab shortcuts

Below is a list of the keyboard shortcuts used to open each of the Ribbon tabs in Microsoft Word.

File = Alt+F
Home = Alt+H
Insert = Alt+N
Page Layout = Alt+P
References = Alt+S
Mailings = Alt+M
Review = Alt+R
View = Alt+W
Acrobat = Alt+B

Closing a Document

Everything that has a beginning indeed has its end. Using Word without closing it is impossible, so let's have recaps on opening the Word, moving around, and closing it for the next time.

When you are through working in a document, you need to close it. This will help prevent unintended changes from being made to it, and also to free the computer's working memory [Random Access Memory (RAM)] some space.

Note, however, that closing a document means simply closing the active document (using the Close command or alternatives), without actually quitting the entire Word window.

There are several ways of closing a document in Word. These methods can be used:

- The File menu

MICROSOFT WORD

- The Close Window button on the menu bar
- Shortcut keys

Closing a Document Using the File Menu
- From the Menu bar, choose File.
- From the File menu, click Close.

Close a Document Using the Close Window Button on the Menu Bar

Simply click the Close Window **(X)** button to the extreme right of the Menu bar. The active document will be closed, leaving the Word program still running. Word or the Office Assistant will prompt you to save your document, if you have unsaved changes in the document.

Close a Document Using Shortcut Keys

To close the current document without exiting Word, you can use any of the following shortcut keys, if you are a keyboard fan:

- Press Ctrl and F4 keys simultaneously on the keyboard (Ctrl + F4).

OR

- Press Ctrl and W keys simultaneously on the keyboard (Ctrl + W).

MICROSOFT WORD

CHAPTER 2

FONT FUN

A Knowledge of Fonts

- A typesetter is someone who sets type on inputs graphics on a page. The process once involved block letters, hot lead, and meticulous craftsmanship. Today, typesetters are considered layout artists. They follow the guidelines set by a graphic designer to create a page of text or, in the digital realm, a web page.

- A graphic designer is someone who chooses elements that look good on a page.

- This list includes typefaces, margins, graphics, and other design elements. The designer and layout artist are often the same person.

- Though typeface is the preferred term; this book uses both typeface and font all through. These days, both terms are interchangeable, though technically not the same.

MICROSOFT WORD

Describing text

You might remember when you learned to write and your teacher handed out ruled paper. You copied letters and words and used the rules (lines) as a guide. Those rules weren't illogically drawn on the page. They come from the history of printed text, where everything has a name and a purpose. See figure 2-1 for detail

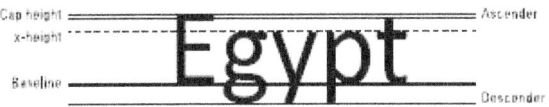

Here are descriptions of the text measurements:

- **Baseline**: Text is written on the baseline.

- **Cap height**: Capital letters extend from the baseline to the cap height.

- **X-height**: Most lowercase letters rise to the x-height, which is named after the lowercase letter x and not anything mysterious.

- **Ascender**: Taller lowercase letters extend to the ascender height.

- **Descender**: Lowercase letters that dip below the baseline drop to the descender.

The purpose of these lines is consistency. Though letters have different shapes and sizes, these rules help the reader absorb the text. When letters disobey the rules, the text becomes more difficult to read.

Text is also measured from side to side. The yardstick that's used is the width of the big M. That measurement is called an **em**. In digital typefaces, the **em square** is a box used for designing typefaces.

Half of an em is an en, which is also the width of the letter N. That measurement isn't as precise as the em, because, in many typefaces, the en isn't exactly half the width of an em.

The two ems make an M&M, which is very pleasing and often crushed in great numbers.

- Grade-school lined paper features the baseline, x-height, and cap height lines.

As you progress through school and even into the workplace, only the baseline remains as a guide, though the other lines still exist in the world of fonts.

- In many fonts, the cap height and ascender are at the same position.

- The x-height can be set high, as shown in Figure 2-1, but often it marks the midpoint between the baseline and cap height. Its location depends on the typeface design.

- Font width varies depending on the font's design, whether the font is heavily weighted, and whether the font is proportionally spaced or monospaced. See the next section for details on these terms.

- A dash, equal in width to the M character is called an em dash. A space equal in width to the M character is an em space.

- The en dash is equal in width to the letter N. An en space is a space of the same width.

- A hyphen is a character, shorter than the en dash.

- Use a hyphen to hyphenate words or as a minus sign.

- The hyphen appears on the PC's keyboard, next to the 0 key on the top row and in the upper right corner of the numeric keypad.

- Use an en dash to specify a range, **such as pages 22–24**.

Understanding text attributes

A font has many attributes, which define the way the font looks and how it can be best put to use. Many of the font attributes are related to Word's text formatting commands. Here's the Big Picture:

Typeface: The font name is called the typeface. Yes, technically, a font is a typeface.

Serif/sans serif: The two styles of typeface are serif and sans serif. A serif is a decoration added to each character, a small line or embellishment. Serifs make text easier to read, so serif typefaces are preferred for body text. Sans serif typefaces lack decorations and are preferred for document titles and headings.

Times New Roman
Serif typeface, proportional

Helvetica
Sans serif typeface, proportional

Courier New
Serif typeface, monospaced

Figure 2-2 illustrates serif and sans serif typefaces.

Proportional/monospaced: A proportionally spaced typeface uses different widths for each letter, so a little I and a big M are different widths. A monospaced typeface features all letters of the same width, as you'd find on a typewriter.

MICROSOFT WORD

Myriad Pro Light   Myriad Pro Light Italic
Myriad Pro Regular   Myriad Pro Italic
Myriad Pro Semibold   *Myriad Pro Semibold Italic*
Myriad Pro Bold   ***Myriad Pro Bold Italic***
Myriad Pro Black   ***Myriad Pro Black Italic***

Typeface weights   Typeface weights & slants

Figure 2-3 illustrates both proportional and monospace typefaces.

Size: Typeface size is measured in points, or units equal to 0.01388 (1/72) of an inch. So, a typeface that is 72 points tall is 1-inch tall. The measurement is made from the typeface's descender to its cap height. On a computer, the size is measured by an em square, which is the width and height of the letter M.

Weight: The weight value is either part of the typeface itself or added as an effect, such as the bold text attribute. But for many fonts, the weight is selected with the typeface, as shown in Figure 2-3.

Slant or slope: A typeface's slope refers to how the text is angled—the most common slope is italic. Oblique text is similar to italic, but subtler. The slant can also tilt to the right, which is more of a text effect than anything you'll commonly see associated with a typeface.

Width: Many typefaces feature condensed or narrow variations. These fonts include the same basic design, but the text looks thin or skinny.

MICROSOFT WORD

Effects: Finally for the effects, it has little to do with the typeface. Word applies these effects to add emphasis or to look cool. See the later section

"Text Effects Strange and Wonderful."

Text on a line can be manipulated to change the way it looks. For example, tracking can be adjusted to scrunch up characters on a line of text. Kerning can be applied to bring letters closer together. Later sections in this chapter describe it in detail.

- Fonts are installed into Windows, not Word. You must access the Control Panel (even in Windows 10), choose the Appearance and Personalization category. You can click the Fonts

   heading to view installed fonts.

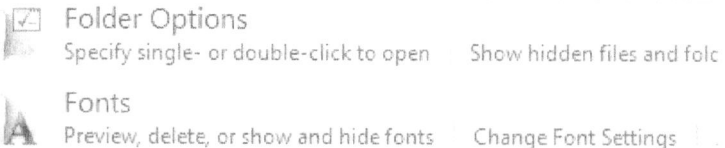

- Fonts are installed on your PC in the Windows\Fonts folder.

- Proportionally spaced typefaces are easier to read.

- Computers traditionally uses monospace fonts for programming and other historically text-only documents. The benefit is that the text's characters line up evenly into columns.

- The old typewriters produced monospace text. The two styles, elite and pica, refer to text approximately 10 points and 12 points tall, respectively. The term pica is also a unit of measurement, equal to 1/6 of an inch — which is 12 points.

- Beyond proportional and monospace, serif and sans serif, typefaces can be scripted, foreign, decorative, ornamental, or a plethora of variations.

- Select a heavy typeface over applying the bold text format. Word may select the heavy typeface automatically when you set the **bold** attribute. The result is that the heavy typeface looks better than when Word attempts to make text look bold.

- Other typeface's weights, not shown in Figure 2-3, include Book, Roman, and Heavy. Still, other variations might be available, depending on how the font is designed and named.

- Italic and oblique text are two different types of slant. Italic is often a specific design, whereas oblique is simply a subtle slant to the standard typeface.

- Just as you should choose a heavy typeface instead of applying the bold text format, if an italic or oblique typeface is available, use it instead of applying the italic text format. See the next section.

Selecting the proper typeface

The general rule for text design is to use sans serif fonts for titles and headings and use serif fonts for document text. Like all rules, this one is broken frequently and deliberately. Even in Word, the default document theme uses sans serif Calibri as both the body text and headings typeface.

If you have trouble choosing fonts, take advantage of the Design tab's document themes in Word. Follow these steps:

- Click the Design tab.

- In the Document Formatting group, select a theme.

Each theme combines typeface elements with colors and other tidbits to help your document maintain its overall appearance.

MICROSOFT WORD

As you point the mouse at various themes, the document's text updates to reflect the theme's attributes.

- Avoid using decorative or ornamental typefaces in your document. They look nifty but makes reading difficult.

- A scripted typeface looks handwritten, and you might feel it adds a personal touch. For a short note, an invitation, or a thank-you card, that typeface works well. For a long document, however, a scripted typeface hinders readability.

- Choosing a new document theme is optional. You can always create your own document styles to set heading and body typefaces.

- Until Word 2007, the normal body text typeface was Times New Roman. The heading typeface was Helvetica or Arial.

Font Control

In Word, the term font is used over typeface, which is inaccurate but acceptable. Don't let the scientific naming system get in the way. The purpose of the Font command is to select the type of text used in your documents.

Exploring the Font group

The first place you most likely go to control text in your document is the Font group on the Ribbon's Home tab. It hosts commands for basic typeface selection and manipulation, as illustrated in Figure 2-4.

Font Specifications and Standards

Beyond typeface and other typographical nonsense, a few digital standards rule the world of computer fonts. You may have heard the names: TrueType and OpenType.

TrueType is a digital font standard, created by Apple and Microsoft. It was designed to compete with Adobe's PostScript fonts, which rendered better on the computer screen back in the early 1990s. **OpenType** is the successor to TrueType, which was developed in the late 1990s.

To determine which font is which, open the Font dialog box. Choose a font, and its type is confirmed below the Preview window.

Other fonts are stirred into the mix and flagged as non-TrueType in Word. These fonts may not look as good as TrueType/OpenType fonts. You may also find that some of Word's advanced text-effect commands don't apply to non-TrueType/OpenType fonts.

MICROSOFT WORD

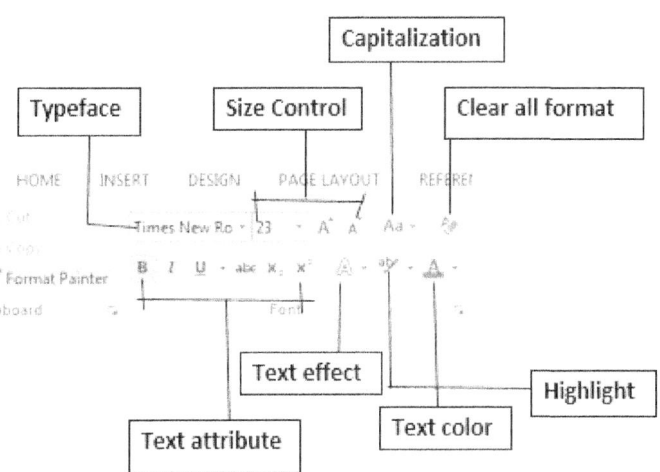

Figure 2-4

The two key items in the Font group set the typeface and text size. Other common attribute commands are available, such as Bold and Italic, as well as commands for text effects, text color, capitalization, and highlighting.

- Text formatting commands in the Font group are applied to any new text you type or to selected text.

- Many of the commands shown in the Font group are echoed on the Mini Toolbar, which appears when you select or right-click text.

- Capitalization and highlighting commands are not text formats or attributes.

They manipulate the way text looks but don't affect the typeface.

- The Clear All Formatting command resets all font attributes and modifications back to the underlying style. So, if the style is Calibri 11-point text, click the option that says ***Clear All Formatting button to restore selected text to that style.***

- The keyboard shortcut for the Clear All Formatting command is Ctrl+spacebar.

Using the Font dialog box

For detailed control over the text format, use the Font dialog box. It offers far more controls than are found on the Ribbon. Follow these steps to bring up the **Font dialog *box*:**

- Click the Home tab.

- In the Font group, click the dialog box launcher.

The Font dialog box is shown in Figure 2-5.

MICROSOFT WORD

And now, the shortcut key: Press Ctrl+D to quickly summon the Font dialog box.

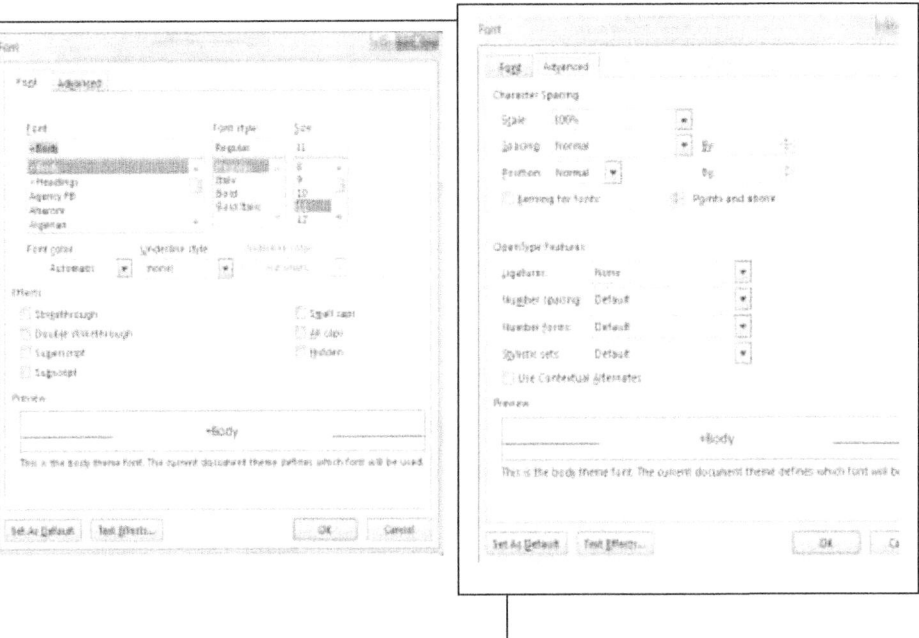

Figure 2-5

The Font tab in the Font dialog box (on the left in Figure 2-5) is the traditional, go-to place for standard text-attribute application and formatting fun. More interesting and unusual text-manipulation commands are found on the Advanced tab (on the right in Figure 2-5).

Even more text effects are available when you click on the Text Effects button illustrated in the figure. These options are discussed in the later section *"Text Effects Strange and Wonderful."*

- Settings made in the Font dialog box are applied to any new text that is typed or to any selected text.

- The Automatic font color (refer to Figure 2-5) is the color set by the current style or the document theme. For the Normal style, the color is black.

- Refer to the next section for information on the +Body and +Headings fonts, shown in the Font dialog box.

Choosing fonts with a theme

To spare you the expense of hiring a graphics designer, Word comes with multiple sets of document themes. These are organized by elements such as heading and body fonts, colors, and effects. The purpose isn't to replace styles, but rather to offer preset combinations that work well together. In fact, you don't need to mess with document themes, if you don't want to.

To view available documents, click the Design tab. Themes are available from the Themes button, which includes all theme elements: fonts, colors, and effects.

The Style Set gallery is used to select specific fonts. Individual theme attributes can be set as well, as illustrated in Figure 2-6.

The Fonts button in the Document Formatting group shows a list of fonts you can choose from to replace the current document theme. These fonts become the *+Body and +Heading fonts, shown in the Fonts dialog box. (Refer to Figure 2-5.)*

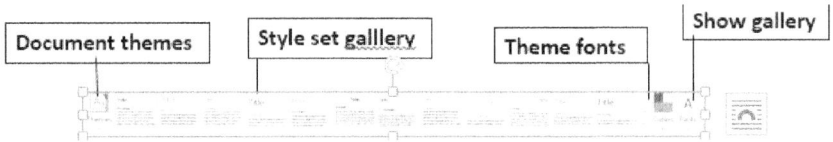

Figure 2-6

Selecting a new font, or any document theme element, immediately affects all aspects of the document if you're using Word's standard styles from the Normal template. If you've set your own styles, theme changes may not have any effect.

Changing the Default Font

The default font is set in the Normal template, which Word uses for any new document without a specific template assigned. The Normal style in the Normal template is preset to match the document theme, but you can change that setting.

Follow these steps:

- Press Ctrl+D.

- The Font dialog box appears.

- Choose the typeface you want to use for all new documents opened in Word.

If ou want to use Times New Roman, you can choose that typeface in the Font dialog box.

- Set the text size.

- Set any additional text attributes.

You probably don't want to set any additional attributes, but if so, do it now.

- Click the button Set As Default.

Word prompts you to indicate whether you want to make the change only for the current document or for all new documents based on the Normal template.

6. Choose the option **All Documents Based On the Normal.dotm Template.**

7. Click **OK.**

From this point onward, all new documents that you create uses the typeface, size and any other attributes you selected.

- To start a new document in Word, press Ctrl+N.

- This change doesn't affect documents that use a template other than Normal.

Typography Control

Word offers some typeface options that go beyond standard text formatting.

These controls let you manipulate the typeface in degrees beyond standard attributes. The modifications allow you to reset the text size, spacing, and position. They also give you permission to hide Text, which is a curious attribute, yet it remains a valid option in Word.

Changing text scale

The **Scale command** changes the text size in a horizontal direction, so it's different from point size, which sets the typeface's overall size. Use the Scale command to fatten or thin your text, making it wider or narrower.

To adjust the width of a chunk of text, follow these directions:

- Select the chunk of Text to modify.

- Press Ctrl+D.

- Click the Advanced tab in the Font dialog box.

- Choose a percentage value from the Scale menu, or type a specific scale.

The larger the percentage, the wider each character becomes.
Use the Preview box in the Font dialog box to get an idea of how the command affects the selected text (from Step 1).

- Now, tap on, OK.

The new width is applied to your text.

For each scale percentage, note that the text height (size in points) remains the same. Only the text's width changes.

- I don't recommend setting the text scale for your document's body text; this type of command is best suited for headings or other document elements where unusually sized text draws attention.

- Setting a very narrow text width is one way to generate a font size that's otherwise too small to produce.

- If the typeface offers a Narrow or Wide variation, use that rather than the Scale command.

- Some typefaces don't scale well at the larger end of the spectrum. You must decide whether a scaled typeface is worth any ugliness generated by the effect.

Setting character spacing

You probably don't think about the spacing between characters, which is exactly what a typeface designer wants. Despite all that talent and effort, Word lets you override the decisions of a typeface designer and reset the amount of space between characters in a line of text.

To condense or expand spaces between each letter, see these steps through:

- Select the text you want to expand or condense.

- Press Ctrl+D to bring up the Font dialog box.

- Click the Advanced tab.

- From the Spacing menu, choose Expand or Condensed to increase or reduce the space between letters in the selected text.

- Manipulate the **by gizmo** to set how wide or narrow or to set the spaces between letters.

- Click OK to set the character spacing.

As with changing the text scale (refer to the preceding section), I recommend manipulating character spacing only for document titles and headings.

Adding kerning and ligatures

To adjust the spaces between specific letters in a typeface, you can apply kerning to the text or use special character combinations known as ligatures.

Kerning is a character-spacing command that involves only specific letters. It scrunches together those characters, such as the A and V, to make the text more readable. To kern text in your document, conside these directions:

- Press Ctrl+D.

The Font dialog box appears.

MICROSOFT WORD

- Click the Advanced tab.

- Place a checkmark by setting Kerning for Fonts.

- Set a text size value in the Points and Above box.

- Click OK

Unlike other items in the Font dialog box, kerning is applied to all text throughout the document, as long as the text's point size is larger than what's set in Step 4.

Another way to make text more readable and decrease the space between certain letters is to apply ligatures. A ligature connects two or more letters, such as the F and I in the Word file. Converting text in this manner is a feature of the OpenType font, so it's not available to all typefaces. If you want to try it, follow these steps:

- Select the chunk of text to which you want to apply a ligature.

- Press Ctrl+D.

- In the File dialog box, click the Advanced tab.

- From the Ligatures menu, choose Standard Only.

If this choice has no effect on the text, choose All.

- Click OK.

The All setting (refer to Step 4) adds just about every ligature possible, which may produce some funky results in the text. If so, consider scaling back your choice to Standard and Contextual.

- Without kerning, some words appear to have extra space in them. Kerning addresses that issue.

- Technically, kerning intrudes upon the integrity of the virtual em square around each character in a digital font. Because kerning is applied only to specific letters, the effect improves readability.

- If you desire to kern all letters on a line of text, adjust the character spacing.

Refer to the preceding section.

- Not every font (typeface) spots ligatures.

- You can also insert ligatures directly. On the Insert tab, choose Symbol and select more Symbols. In the Symbol dialog box, the **fi and fl** ligatures are found in the Symbol dialog box, under the subset Alphabetic Presentation Forms.

Adjusting text position

The two basic text-positioning commands are Superscript and Subscript, found in the Home tab's Font group. These commands allow you to reduce the text size and shift the baseline up or down to create subscripts such as H20 and superscripts such as **E=mc2**. You can apply a similar effect to your text by shifting the baseline up or down, as illustrated in Figure 2-7.

MICROSOFT WORD

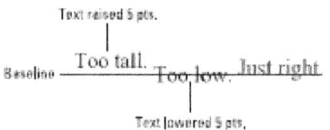

Figure 2-7

To adjust text position above or below the baseline, heed these directions:

- Select the text you want raised or lowered.

Ensure that it's a small chunk of text. Raising an entire line of text would be impractical.

- Press Ctrl+D to bring forth the Font dialog box.

- Click the Advanced tab.

- From the Position menu, choose **Raised or Lowered.**

- Select a point value from the **By gizmo**.

For example, to raise a word 3 points from the baseline, choose Raised and then 3 pt from the box.

- Click OK to apply the new text position.

To remove raised or lowered text, repeat these steps and choose Normal in Step 4, and then click OK.

- Raising or lowering text can affect line spacing within a paragraph as well as spacing between paragraphs. If you have paragraph line spacing at the exact setting, the text may bump the line above or below. See Chapter 5 for more information on paragraph line spacing.

- The Subscript command button is shown in the margin. Its keyboard equivalent is **Ctrl+=**. Use this command to subscript a single character of text.

- The Superscript command button is shown in the margin. Its keyboard equivalent is Ctrl+Shift+=. This command is preferred when you want to superscript a single character.

Text Effects Strange and Wonderful

If you really want to have fun with fonts, you can apply some of Word's text effects. These aren't typeface attributes, but rather special effects applied to a font. And like all strange and wonderful things in the world of fonts, these effects are best suited for headings and titles, not for body text.

The WordArt command is a great shortcut to stick interesting text into your document. For most fancy text times, choosing this command saves you a lot of time and frustration.

Accessing the Format Text Effects pane

To apply text effects, you need to open up the Format Text Effects pane, illustrated in Figure 2-8.

To display this pane, follow these steps:

- Press Ctrl+D to bring forth the Font dialog box.

- Click the Text Effects button.

The button is found near the lower left corner of the dialog box. If it's disabled, the current typeface cannot be manipulated.

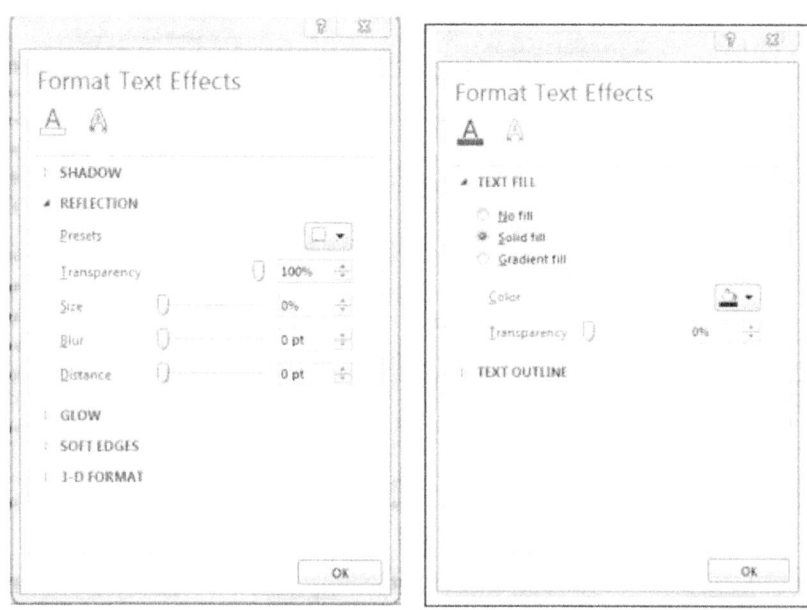

Figure 2-8

The Format Text Effects pane features two tabs, illustrated in Figure 2-8. The left tab handles text fill and outline options. The right tab lists a host of effects.

Each item in the Format Text Effects pane is collapsible. Click the triangle to expand the item; click again to collapse, as illustrated in Figure 2-8.

To make adjustments, select the text you want to format. Work the pane to apply the effects, which, sadly, cannot be previewed. After making adjustments, click the OK button to apply, and then click OK again to close the Font dialog box.

Changing text fill

The Font dialog box, as well as the Font group on the Home tab, features the Font Color button. To apply color to the font's outline as well as use more than just a solid color, you access the Text Fill area of the Format Text Effects pane; refer to Figure 2-8.

The Solid Fill option works like the Font Color command: Choose Solid Fill and select a color. Use the Transparency slider to add a transparent, or ghost effect to the text.

When you choose Gradient Fill, the pane changes to show many more controls. The options available for Gradient Fill are numerous. The key is the **Gradient Stops bar**, which features

MICROSOFT WORD

different color settings at different positions. The settings blend along the bar to build the gradient pattern.

Here are the general steps taken to create a gradient fill pattern:

- Select the Text.

Gradient fill works best on titles and perhaps on a caption or another graphical element. It would look horrid if applied to a heading or body text.

- Press Ctrl+D.

- Click the Text Effects button in the Font dialog box.

- Click the Fill and Outline tab on the Format Text Effects pane.

Refer to Figure 2-8 for the tab's location.

- Expand the Text Fill area.

- Choose Gradient Fill.

- Select a fill from the Preset Gradients button or create your own fill.

- Click OK to apply the fill, and then click OK again to close the Font dialog box.

If you opt to create your own fill (refer to Step 7), you can set two or more stops on the Gradient Stops bar, to select a color for each stop:

Click on the bar to set a stop, and then choose a color from the Color button menu.

To remove a stop, use the mouse to drag it from the Gradient Stops bar. You can also use the Remove Stop and Add Stop buttons.

Four types of gradients are available, as chosen from the Type menu. You will see a Radial gradient, which fans out from a center point. The Position box is what sets the center point. Use the Direction button to see how the gradient is applied to the text. Unfortunately, the Gradient Settings changes aren't previewed live in your document.

The best way to see the effect is to click OK. Use the Preview portion of the Font dialog box to check your work.

Setting a text outline

A font has both a fill color and an outline color. The Font Color command affects only the fill, not the outline. To add an outline or a border to text, you apply the Text Outline effect.

Pay attention to these steps to add a text outline:
- Select the text.

The text doesn't need to work to have a fill color; the Automatic color (usually, black) works fine. You can, however, set **No Fill** as the text color, in which case only the outline shows up.

- Press Ctrl+D and click the Text Effects button in the Font dialog box.

- Ensure that the Fill and Outline tab is chosen in the Format Text Effects pane.

- Expand the Text Outline area.

- Choose Solid Line or Gradient Line to set the type of outline.

For Gradient Line, you can configure the gradient color stops and other options, as discussed in the preceding section.

- Use the Width gizmo to set the outline width.

Width is measured in points. Larger values show a heavier outline.

- Set other options to customize how the line looks.

- Click OK, and then click OK again to view your effects.

The text modifications may not show up in the Font dialog box's Preview window, so you must return to the document to view your efforts.

In Step 7 you can further manipulate the line's look, depending on which line attribute you choose:

Compound Type: Use the Compound Type menu to choose line styles, such as a double line, thick and thin lines, and more.

Dash Type: The Dash Type menu sets whether the line is solid or composed of dashes or dots in various patterns and lengths.

Cap Type: Items on the Cap Type menu set how the border goes around a curve.

The options are Square, Round, and Flat; this effect doesn't really show up unless the text is quite large or the outline is thick.

Join Type: The Join Type menu determines what happens when lines meet. As with the cap type, this effect requires large text or thick lines to show up.

As with other settings in the Format Text Effects pane, you must set your options and then click OK to view the results in the Font dialog box.

Creating hidden Text

Perhaps the **strangest font** attribute is the hidden text. You won't find this setting in the Format Text Effects dialog box, because it's more of a deception than an effect: What's the point of writing something that doesn't show up on the screen or in a printed

MICROSOFT WORD

document? I honestly can't think of any proper situation, but the command is available.

To hide text, follow these steps:

- Select the text you want to disappear.

The text isn't deleted; it's merely hidden.

- Press Ctrl+D to summon the Font dialog box.

- Place a check mark by the Hidden item.

The Hidden item is found on the Font tab in the Effects area.

- Click OK and the Text is hidden.

Now that the text is hidden, the big question is, ***"How do, I get it back?"*** In fact, how do you even find the Text?

The easy way to view hidden text is to use the Show/Hide command, located on the Home tab in the Paragraph group. Its icon is shown in the margin. Click the button, and the hidden text appears in the document with a dotted underline.

You can also direct Word to show hidden text all the time. Consider these steps:

- Click the File tab.

- Choose Options.

The Word Options dialog box appears.

- Choose Display from the list of categories on the left side of the dialog box.

- In the **Always Show** area, place a checkmark by the option **Hidden Text**

- and click OK.

Though you can make hidden text visible, it doesn't print unless you direct Word to also print the hidden text. To do so, repeat steps 1 through 3 in the preceding list, but also place a check mark by the item **Print Hidden Text**.

Then again, if you're going to show and print hidden Text, why hide it in the first place?

- Hidden text affects document proofing. That's because the proofing tools (spelling and grammar) ignore the hidden Text.

- I suppose one reason to hide text is that you might want to bring it up later. I wouldn't use this option as an editing tool, but rather as a way to customize a single document for multiple purposes. For example, you might hide more technical information so that you can provide a shorter document as an executive summary.

- Hidden text is used on web pages to conceal various elements. For example, a web page template may list an item that's unused on a page, in which case it can be hidden to avoid confusion.

- The Hidden text attribute isn't the same as the Clear All Formatting command. That command resets any added text attributes to their settings as defined in the underlying style. So, if the style is Normal, the Clear All formatting command removes any applied text formats that aren't part of the Normal style.

- To unhide Text, you must remove the Hidden format: Repeat the first step listed in this section but in Step 3 remove the check mark (or ensure that the box is blank). You can also use the **Clear All Formatting** command (Ctrl+spacebar), but that removes all text attributes, which may not be what you want.

Find and Replace Text Formatting

One item that relates to fonts but has nothing to do with aesthetics is Word's capability to find and replace fonts and text formatting.

Using this variation of the standard **Find and Replace command** is tricky, **so pay attention!**

To replace formatting, you must add and then subtract the text attributes. Before diving in, I have some bits of advice:

- If you use styles, it's easier to modify a style than to entirely search-and-replace a text format. That's the best way to change an underlying typeface or text size.

- When you find and replace a text format, you must search for the first text format, and then replace it with the second format while removing the first; this sounds odd, which is why if you try this type of operation on your own, it might fail.

- Always remove the formatting attributes from the Find and Replace dialog box when you're done. If you don't, Word would continue searching for text attributes, which may limit future searches.

Obey these steps to find and replace a text attribute, such as underline with italics:

- Press Ctrl+Home to position the insertion pointer at the tippy-top of the document.

MICROSOFT WORD

- Press Ctrl+H to bring up the Find and Replace dialog box, with the replace tab forward.

- Click the More button to expand the Find and Replace dialog box.

- Click the **Find What text** box, but leave it blank.

- Click the Format button and choose Font from the menu.

The Font dialog box appears.

- Select the format you want to find.

For example, click the Underline Style button and choose the single underline.

- Click OK to close the Font dialog box and return to the Find and Replace dialog box.

- Click the Replace text box and leave it blank.

9. Click the Format button and choose Font.

The Font dialog box appears again.

10. From the Font Style list, choose Italics.

11. From the Underline Style menu, choose None.

These two steps (10 and 11) carry out the important task of not only selecting the replacement text format but also removing the

MICROSOFT WORD

original text format. In this example, you're choosing underline and replacing it with no underline and italics.

12. Click OK to close the Font dialog box.

13. The Search and Replace dialog box should look similar to Figure 2-9.

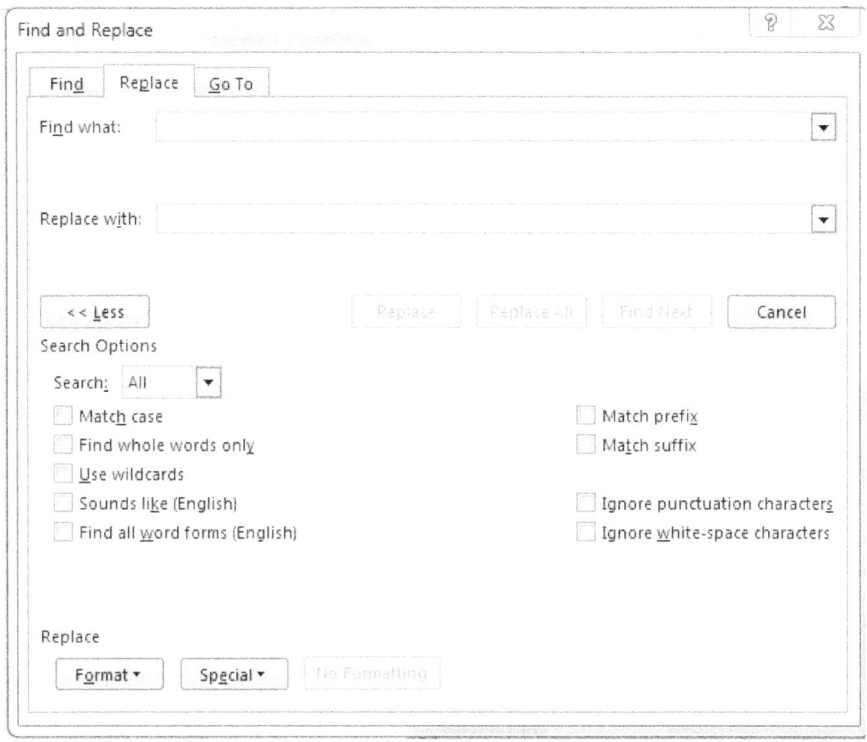

Figure 2-9

14. Click the Replace All button to search and replace the text attribute throughout the document.

A summary box appears, listing the number of replacements made.

15. Click OK to dismiss the summary.

Now comes the important steps of removing the formatting attributes.

16. Click the **Find What text box** and click the **No Formatting** button.

17. Click the **Replace With text box** and click the **No Formatting** button.

These steps (16 and 17) remove formatting options from the next find-and-replace operation. That way, these options won't mess up the next search or search-and-replace operation.

18. Click the Close button to dismiss the Find and Replace dialog box.

If you were to replace italics with underline, you'd need to search for the Italic text style and replace it with the regular text style as well as the single-underline format. If you forget to remove the original text format, you end up with double formats instead of a search-and-replace.

You cannot use the steps in this section to peel away text effects. The Text Effects button isn't available in the Font dialog box you activated in Steps 5 and 9.

Thank you for following. Let's move on to the next chapter!!!

MICROSOFT WORD

CHAPTER 3

PAGE FORMATTING

Understanding how page formatting work is essential; hence, this chapter is designed to guide you on any possible trick you might need. At the end of this chapter, it would be great if you're equipped with some mastery skill in the following:

- That you can open the Page Setup dialog box by double-clicking the ruler.

- That every document page has three main independent areas: the Header, the Footer, and the space between the margins.

- That everything you put in the Header will appear on all document pages that has this header.

- How to professionally format a Microsoft Word document to produce nice PDF files.

- How to use the File ➤ Export to PDF/XPS tool and its Options dialog box to create PDF files that use document Headings to create PDF Bookmarks.

- How to take advantage of Microsoft Multiple pages option found in the **Page Setup** dialog box **Margins tab** to produce nice formatting.

- How to use the **Sheets per booklet** option to produce different booklet styles using a four-page signature.

Page Formatting

Microsoft Word pages are easy to configure once you understand how it works and can differentiate the types and usage.

In this chapter, you will learn how to make the most from the Page Setup dialog box and use the page Header and Footer areas to achieve better results in your document formatting and exporting. You will learn how to create and manage different Header and Footer types, insert page numbers (and page count) correctly, and produce nicely formatted e-books, PDF files, and booklet printing using Microsoft Word options.

Types of Documents

Text documents differ from one another in the types of pages they use, and for the sake of this discussion; they can be considered as

- Single-page documents: print on just one side of the paper and one or two types of pages: the first page and the others.

- Mirror page documents: print on both page sides and have two or three types of pages: the first page, odd pages (front), and even pages (back).

- Complex documents: may have different types of pages, changing which side of the paper they print on and presenting different page sizes and orientations.

Microsoft Word deals with page variability inside any text document using the Page Setup dialog box (and its three tabs) to configure the pages. The hidden Section breaks character to indicate where the one-page type begins and end.

The first step to master how to format different page sizes is to understand the Page Setup dialog box and how each document page is constituted.

Page Setup

Whenever a new and blank document in Microsoft Word is opened, you receive a new blank page.

The size of this Page is associated to the page size defined in your default printer. So the first action to produce any printed document is to configure its page size: the medium in which it will be printed and becomes alive.

This is done using one of these methods:

- Using the Size command found in the Page Setup area of the Layout tab to select one of the already set-up page sizes (Figure 3-1).

MICROSOFT WORD

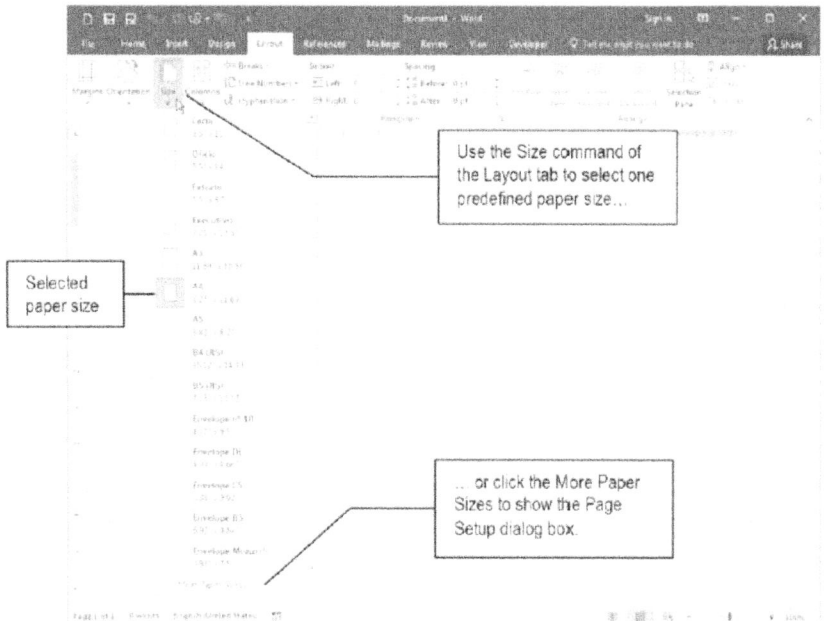

Figure 3-1. Use the Size command found in the Page Setup area of the Layout tab to select a predefined paper size or click on More Paper Sizes... to show the Page Setup dialog box

- Using the Page Setup dialog box, which can be shown by different methods:
- Double-clicking the ruler (the easiest way).
- Using the Size➤ More Paper Sizes... command found in the Page Setup area of the Layout tab.
- Clicking the small Page Setup button found in the Page Setup area of the Layout tab.
- Now, use the File➤ Print➤ Margins➤ Custom Margins command.

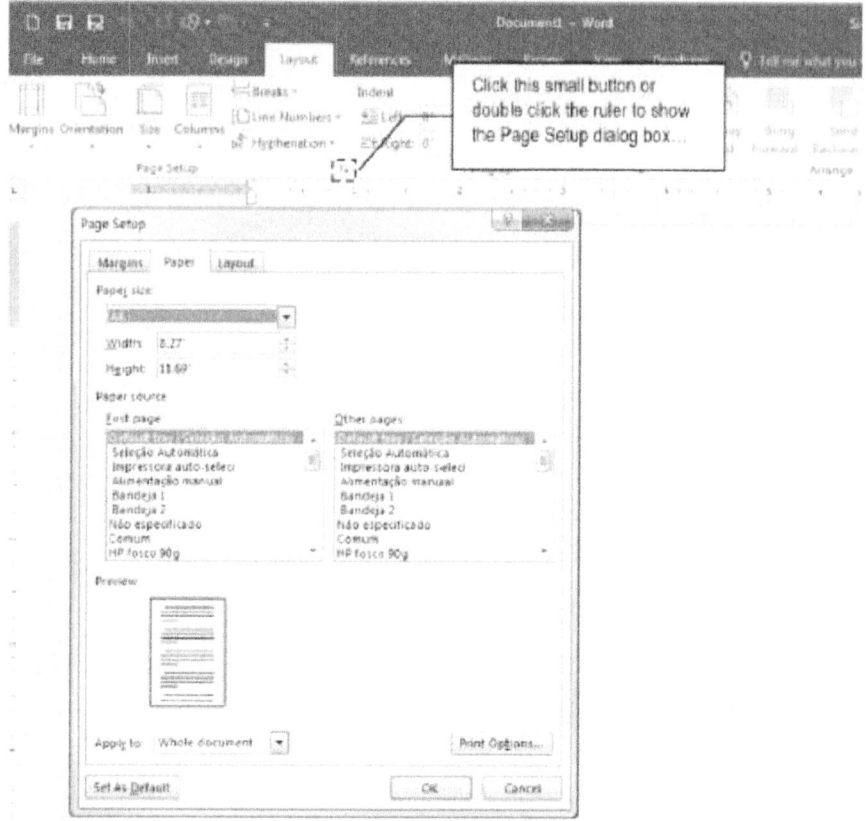

Using any of these methods, you can change the options or show the Page Setup dialog box with the Paper tab selected (Figure 3-2), from where you use the Paper size area to select any of the page sizes presented by the **Layout tab Size command** (see Figure 3-1) or use the Width and Height text boxes to create a Custom Size.

Figure 3-2. Double-click the ruler or click the small button located on the bottom right side of the Page Setup area of the Layout tab to show the Page Setup dialog box with the Paper tab selected.

Attention: The Paper tab also allows selection of the printer tray used by the first Page and other pages of the current document. Paper orientation is selected in the Margins tab.

Once you have defined the paper size, it is time to adjust the document's margins and header and footer sizes.

Margins, Header, and Footer

As seen in any other text-processing software, every Microsoft Word page has three main areas:

- Margins and the space inside them (where the document prints).
- Header: the space above top margin.
- Footer: the space below the bottom margin.

The text you type in any Microsoft Word document will appear inside the document margins of each document page, but whatever you type or insert in the Header or Footer areas will appear on every document page (that is why the Headers and Footers are used to convey document information like page number, page count, date printed, etc.).

Microsoft Word hides these areas from your eyes but you can get a hint about the size of these areas by:

- Using the horizontal and vertical ruler.
- Setting two options found in the Show Document Content area of the **Advanced option** found in Word Options dialog box (File ➤ Options ➤ Advanced):
- Show text boundaries

- Show crop marks.

Attention: It is not obvious to most people that both the Header and Footer are special document page areas, because everything you put in them will appear on every document page. They are mostly used to convey the page number, page count (page n of m), or other document information, like printed date, produced by, and so on.

Figure 3-3 shows how the white Page looks when Crop marks are shown (appearing at the top left and bottom right page corners). It also shows the text boundary around the first empty page paragraph (with the Show/Hide tool checked so you can see the hidden Paragraph break character).

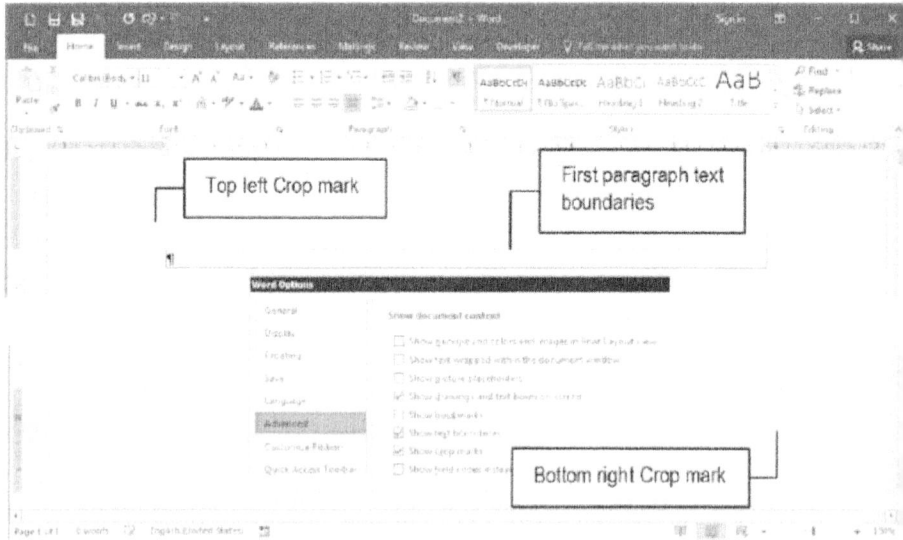

Figure 3-3. The white Page of a new Microsoft Word document showing Crop mark and Text boundary options set for its first paragraph. These options allow you to set the positions of the Header, Footer, and Page margins (top, left, right, and bottom margins).

Accessing the Header and Footer Page Areas

There is more than one way to access the document page Header and Footer areas:

- Double-click the Header and Footer area (identify it by the dark gray area of the ruler, which is above the top crop mark or below the bottom crop mark).

- Use the Header➤ Edit Header (or Footer➤ Edit Footer) commands found in the Header and Footer area of the Insert tab Ribbon.

Whenever you access the Header or Footer area, Microsoft Word activates its content and deactivates the document content (the text of which becomes grayed), while it also activates and shows the Header & Footer Tools Design tab on the Ribbon, where you will find tools to manipulate this special document page area (Figure 3-4).

MICROSOFT WORD

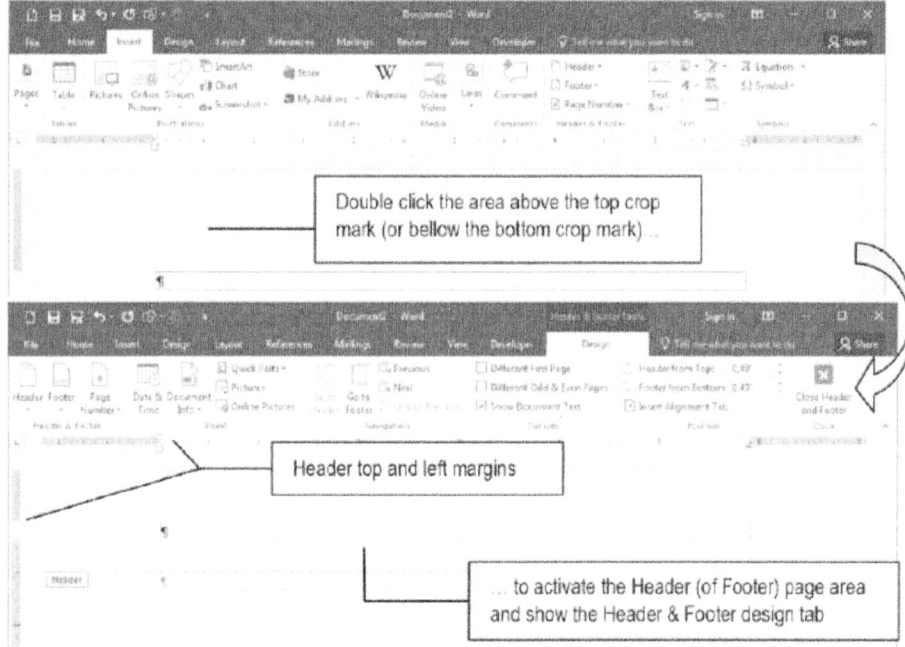

Figure 3-4. Double-click the page area above (or below) the top (or bottom) crop mark to activate the page Header (or Footer). Microsoft Word will show the Header & Footer Design tab where you can find tools to manipulate this important document page area.

Once the page Header or Footer area is activated, you can alternate between the Header and Footer areas using the Goto Footer (or Goto Header) commands found in the Navigation area of the Header & Footer Tools Design tab of the Ribbon (Figure 3-5).

MICROSOFT WORD

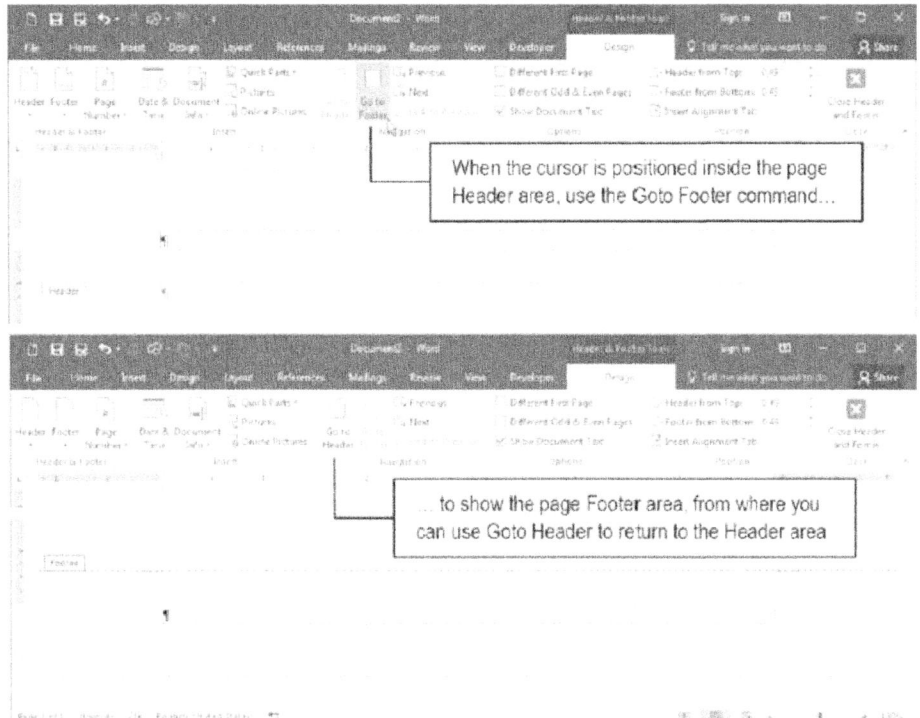

Figure 3-5. To alternate between the page Header and Footer areas, use the Goto Footer and Goto Header commands found in the Navigation area of the Header & Footer Tools Design tab on the Ribbon

Change Page Margin Size

Now that you know that the document page has the special areas called Margins, Header, and Footer, it is interesting to note that Microsoft Word has a dark gray area on its horizontal and vertical rulers to define the space used by its Left, Right, Top, and Bottom page margins, which also appear in the Header and Footer areas.

Since the Page is the same for the entire document, whenever you change its margins, the entire document will obey these new margin values. And once more, this can be done in three different ways:

- setting Page, Header, and Footer margin sizes interactively, by dragging its Ruler guides (Left, Right, Top, and Bottom).
- Using the Layout, the Header and Footer Tools tabs.
- Using the Page setup dialog box.

Formatting E-books

Many people ask how to format a document in Microsoft Word so it can be used by an e-book reader (like the popular Amazon Kindle). It is important to know that this is more a matter of text formatting; there's no need to bother with the page setup applied to the Microsoft Word document, because e-reader devices are quite variable in screen size and resolution.

In general, you must follow these formatting rules to create good-quality Microsoft Word documents that will be nicely read on most e-book devices:

- Body text: Font is unimportant because each reader has its own fonts. Format the Normal style with 10 pt size and a System font like Arial, Times New Roman, or Calibri. Paragraph alignment is unimportant because most e-readers use Left alignment. To detach each paragraph, apply a First line indent = 0.2 or a Space After = 6 pt size and Line spacing = single.
- Title, subtitle and section titles: Must be formatted with Title and Subtitle and the Heading styles, which must be no

larger than 16 pt size. Heading1 can have a Page break before option set.
- Bold, Italic, Underline, and font formatting can be used at will.
- Header and Footer: Must be removed like in any new blank document.
- Page size, Margins, and Alignment: Must not be taken into account because these values will be ignored by the e-book converter.
- Table of Contents: Must be generated using the Custom Table of Contents command with the Show page number option unchecked (index entries must not be followed by page numbers; since page size is variable, page numbers do not make sense).

Once the document is correctly formatted you must save it on the disk and use an e-book converter software (like Calibre, GooReader, 2EPUB, etc.) to convert it to some popular e-book formats, like epub (preferred document format for Android and iOS devices, Kobo eReader, Barnes & Noble Nook, and Amazon Kindle Fire) or the also popular MOBI format (preferred document type for Kindle devices).

Changing the Document Layout

A Microsoft Word document can print differently according to the selections made in the Layout tab of the Page Setup dialog box (Figure 3-6).

- Section: This option allows configuration of what type of section this Page belongs to. Normally a document has just one section which begins on a new page (default option).
- Different odd and even: allows defining if the odd and even pages should have different Header and Footer areas (which is desirable in documents that will be printed on both sides of the paper).
- Different first Page: allows defining if the first document (or section) page will have a different Header and Footer area.

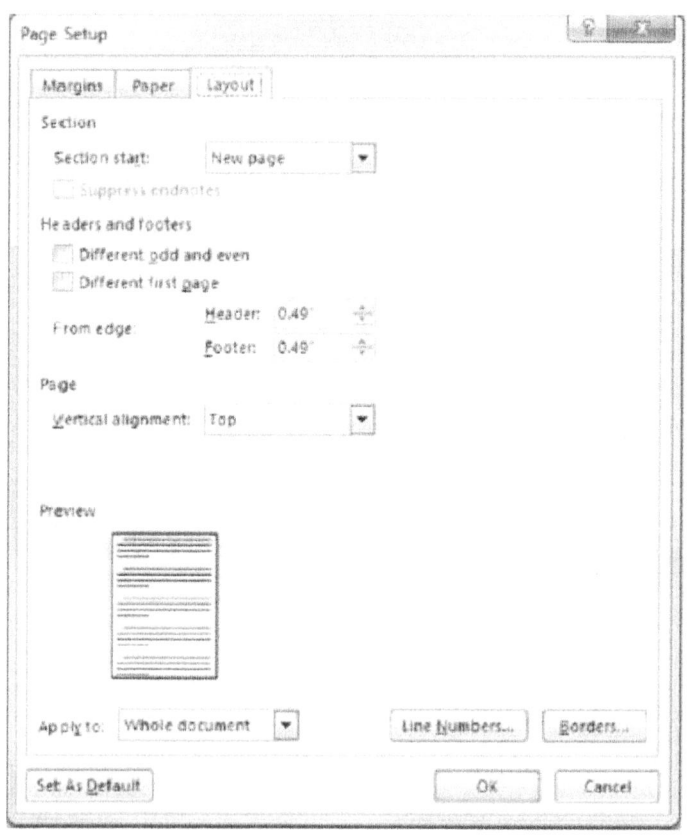

Figure 3-6. Use the Layout tab of the Page Setup dialog box to configure how Microsoft Word manages the document page Header and Footer and the vertical alignment of the text

• From edge: use the Header and Footer options to change the top margin or distance from page edge for the Header and Footer areas (as you can do this by dragging their top handles on the vertical ruler or by changing the Header from the top or Footer from the bottom options found in the Header and Footer Design tab, see Figures 3-4 and 3-5).

• Vertical alignment: define how the text will be vertically aligned on each Page of this document section. Default is Top, meaning that the text begins to print on the top page margin (you can select center bottom or Justify vertical alignments).

Header and Footer for Normal Documents

For the sake of this discussion a Normal document is one formatted with **Multiple Pages** = **Normal** in the Margin tab of the Page Setup dialog box, intended to be printed using the front of the Page.

Figure 3-7 shows Normal documents A, B, C, and D, which have different numbering options (and consequently different types of pages) according to the state of the **Different odd and even,** and **Different first page** options found in the Page Setup dialog box Layout options:

• Document A: pages numbered on the top right side of the Page (single Page with a Header)

• Document B: pages numbered and alternating the top left and top right side of the pages (two page types, with an Odd Page Header and an Even Page Header)

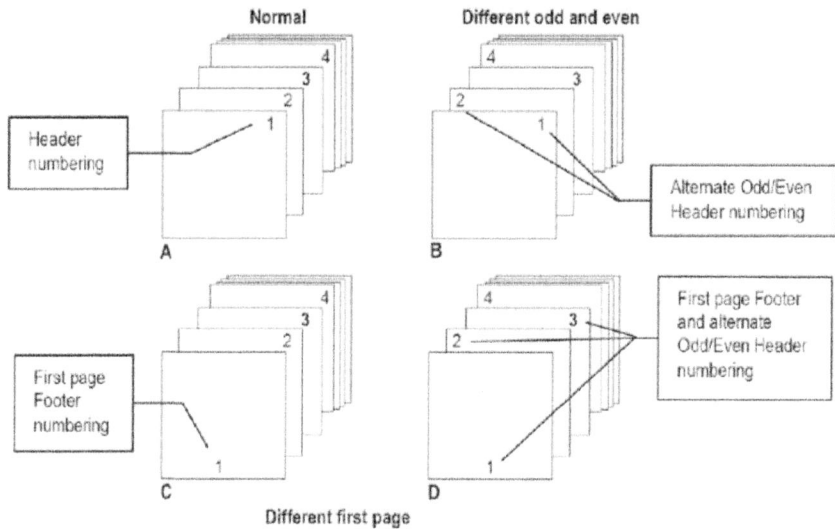

Figure 3-7. Normal document types (A, B, C, and D) numbered according to the state of the Different odd and even Layout option (right column) and the Different first page option (lower row)

• Document C: first Page numbered on Footer (center aligned). All others numbered on the top right side of the Page (two page types, with a First Page Header and a Header)

• Document D: first Page numbered on Footer (center aligned). All other pages numbered and alternating the top left and top right side of the pages (three page types, with a First Page Header and an Odd Page Header and an Even Page Header)

You can reproduce such behavior in Microsoft Word following the next steps:

1. In a new Microsoft Word document, double-click the ruler to show the Page Setup dialog box and format a small page size of 2 × 2, with 0.2 margins all around.

2. Close the Page Setup dialog box and press Ctrl+Enter twice to insert two hidden Page break characters (the document must have two pages).

3. Show the document Header area (double-click the top page area) to activate it and show the Header and Footer Design tab.

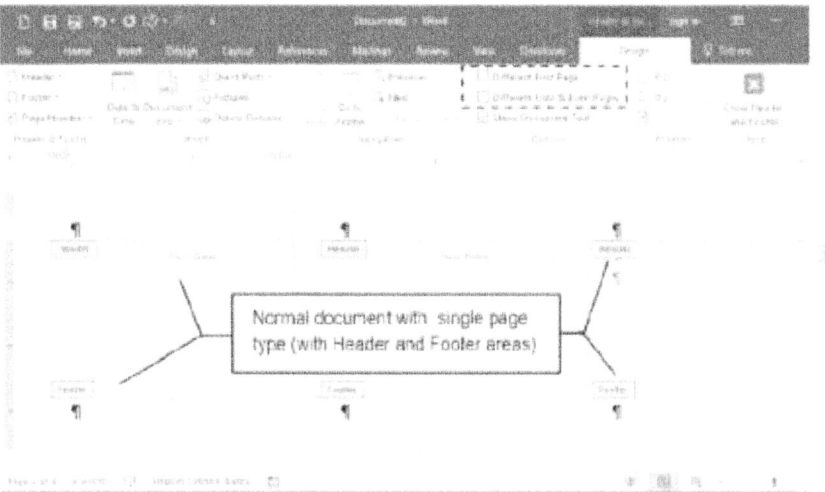

4. Note that the document has just one type of Page (with a Header and Footer area, Figure 3-8).

Figure 3-8. A normal document with two page breaks and a single type of Page has just a Header and a Footer area

5. Check the Different first page options located in the Options area of the Header and Footer Design tab and note that the first Page now has the First Page Header and First Page Footer areas,

while all other pages have the Header and Footer areas (Figure 3-9).

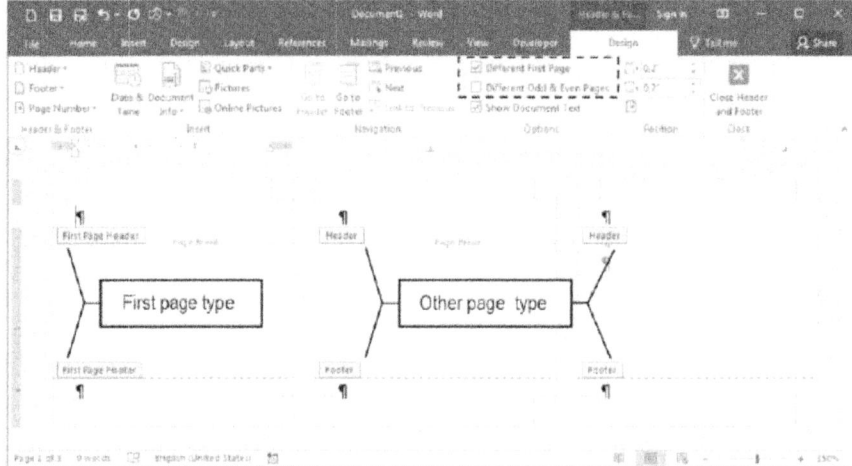

Figure 3-9. A normal document with the Different first page option set has the First Page Header and First Page Footer areas on its first Page, while all other pages have just the Header and Footer areas

6. Check the Different Odd & Even Pages options located in the Options area of the Header and Footer Design tab and note that now the document has on its first Page the First Page Header and First Page Footer areas, on its second Page, the Even Page Header and Even Page Footer, and on its third Page the Odd Page Header and Odd Page Footer areas (Figure 3-10).

MICROSOFT WORD

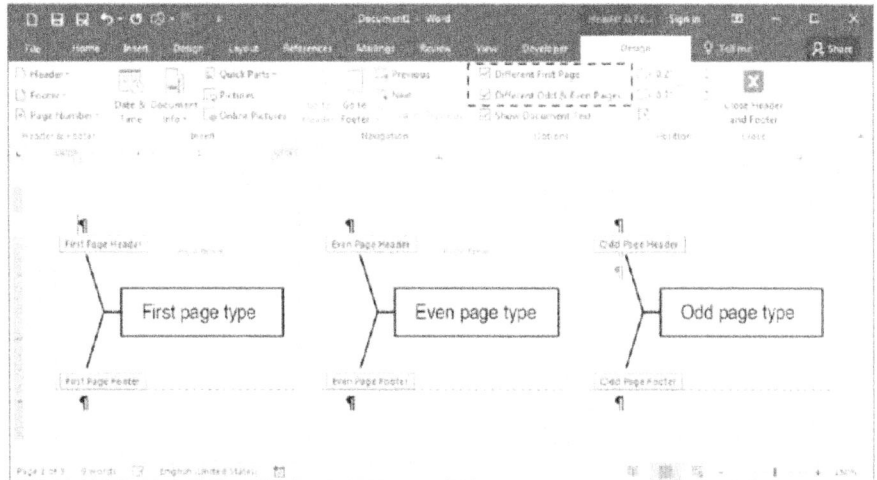

Figure 3-10. When the Different First Page and Different Odd & Even Pages options found in the Options area of the Header and Footer Design tab are checked, a normal document will have three different page types: the first Page, the even pages, and the odd pages.

Follow these tips to navigate to the different types of pages produced by the Different first Page and Different Odd & Even Pages options using the Navigation area of the Header & Footer Design tab tools:

• When the Header is activated and selected, use the Go To Footer button to select the Footer of the same Page (vice versa with the Go To Header button).

• Press the Next button to go forward on the different page Headers or Footers.

• Press the Previous button to go backward on the different page Headers or Footers.

- Keep the Show document text selected to see the document text grayed (deactivated) when the Header/Footer is activated.

Formatting PDF Files

PDF—Portable Document Format—is an industry standard created by Adobe to generate electronic read-only documents that can be opened by Adobe Reader, Fox Reader, Nitro PDF Reader, PDF-Xchange Editor, and many other free software packages available on the Internet.

Although you print a PDF file from any Microsoft Windows program by installing and using a PDF Printer program (like CutePDF, DoPDF, PDFCreator, etc.), Microsoft Word can easily create PDF documents using its File ➤ Export command (which also allows you to create an XDF file).

Attention XDF is the XML version of a PDF file, which was once supposed to become the most used electronic, read-only file type—a forecast that has been confirmed so far.

In general, you must follow these formatting rules to create good-quality PDF files from Microsoft Word documents:

1. Use a popular page format (like Letter or A4).
2. Use Heading styles (Heading1 to Heading9) to format chapter and section titles.
3. Add Header and Footer information for the first Page, odd and even pages to:
   - Identify the document title on each Page.
   - Add page number and page count to each Page.

MICROSOFT WORD

By using Heading styles, you can use Microsoft Word File➤ Export command and click the Create PDF/XPS button to show the Publish as PDF or XPS dialog box and define the PDF options desired (Figure 3-11).

Figure 3-11. Use Microsoft Word File➤ Export➤ Create PDF/XPS Document to show the Publish as PDF or XPX dialog

box. ***Click Options and select Create bookmarks using Headings option to create the PDF Table of Contents (Bookmarks).***

The Create PDF/XPS Option dialog box offers these options:

- **Standard (publishing online and printing)**: document receives the best quality output.

- **Minimum size (publish online)**: document receives minimum image quality settings.

- **Options**: use this button to show the PDF Options dialog box, from where you can use:

- Page Range area: decide which pages must be exported to the PDF file.

- Publish what: only document text or text and markups (if any).

- Include nonprinting information:

- Create bookmarks using: select Headings to use Heading styles to create the PDF Table of Contents.

- Document Properties: save all document properties in PDF, like author name, date created, etc.

- Document structure tags for accessibility: tags are for accessibility; they indicate the structure of a document so it can be read for persons with disabilities. They communicate the reading order and determine exactly which items will be read.

- **_PDF Options:_**
  - PDF/A Compliant: PDF/A is a new electronic document standard that guarantee that the final PDF will preserve its visual appearance over time and independent of the tools that will be used in the future to open it.
  - Bitmap text when fonts may not be embedded: convert text to bitmap when it is not possible to insert the font information in the document.
  - Encrypt document with a password: protect the document with a password, which will be needed to open and read it.

Attention: Whenever your document has Heading styles applied to its chapter and section titles, it defines the Create bookmarks = Headings. This will make the PDF reader software exhibit the Bookmarks pane, from where you can navigate through the PDF document just like you do when using Microsoft Windows Navigation Pane Headings view.

Formatting Booklets

The term Booklet is usually attributed to a small book made up of 40 pages, where each sheet of paper is printed on front and back, receiving two pages on each paper side (constituting what is called a four-page signature), usually having an outer cover page made up of paperboard (or any other paper of bigger grammage).

To compose a booklet, we can print these four-page sheet signatures and;

- Individually fold them in the middle, composing a notebook of one sheet of paper; the booklets are then stacked in the right order, receiving staples or spirals to bind the booklets, or;
- Stack each four-page signature in the right order, and fold the stacked sheets in the middle to compose a single notebook that is then stapled together to bind the booklet.

Attention: A variation of this process is to create notebooks of up to ten stacked four-page signatures folded in the middle, which are stacked with other similar notebooks that will be spiral-bound to compose the final booklet.

Microsoft Word creates booklets by printing sheet signatures of four document pages, choosing which document pages will be printed on each sheet's signature side according to the **Sheets per page** option that appears whenever you set Multiple Pages options to Book Fold (found in the Page Setup dialog box, Margins tab, Figure 3-12).

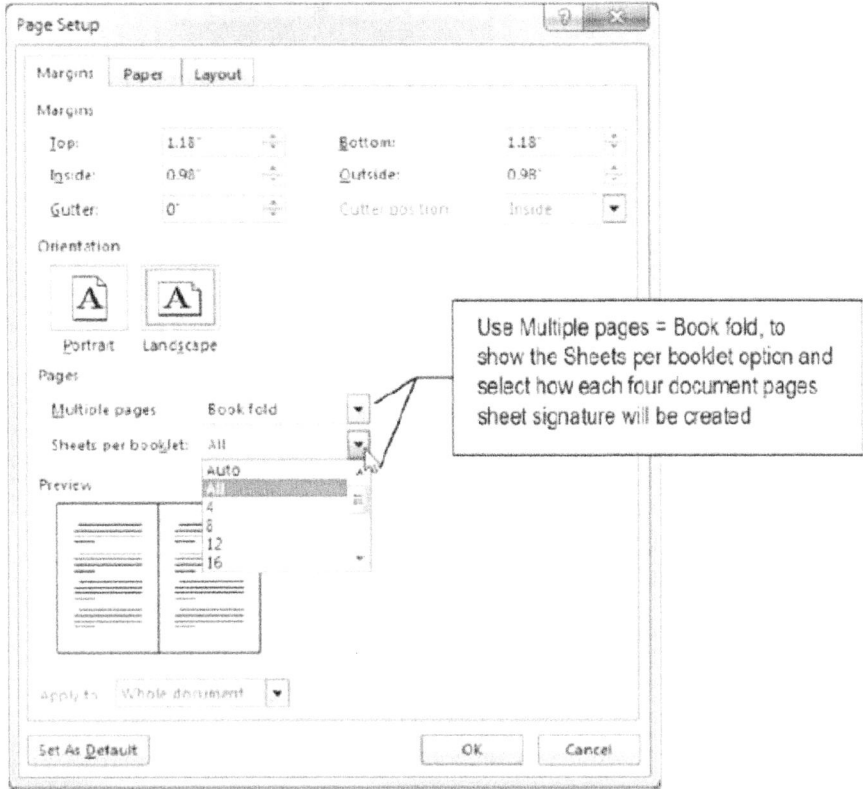

Figure 3-12. Whenever you select Multple pages = Book fold in the Margins tab of the Page Setup dialog box, Microsoft Word will show the Sheets per booklet option to allow selection of how each sheet signature of four document pages will be created.

The Sheets per booklet options are as follows:

• **All**: default value, includes all document pages to compose the sheet signatures, which needs to be stacked and folded in the middle to compose the final booklet.

• **Auto**: includes up to 40 successive document pages to compose notebooks of up to ten sheet signatures (of four pages each), which need to be stacked and folded in the middle. The notebooks will then be stacked together to compose the final booklet.

- **4**: use four successive document pages to compose sheet signatures that create notebooks of single sheets of paper. The single-page notebooks are then stacked together to compose the final booklet.
- **8**: uses eight successive document pages to compose sheet signatures, which create notebooks of two successive sheets of paper that need to be stacked together and folded in their middle. The two-page notebooks are then stacked together to compose the final booklet.
- **12** to **40**: indicates the number of successive sheet signatures that will create notebooks of a multiple of four sheets of paper that need to be stacked together and folded in their middle (12 = 3 sheet signatures, 16 = 4 sheet signatures, 40 = 10 sheet signatures).

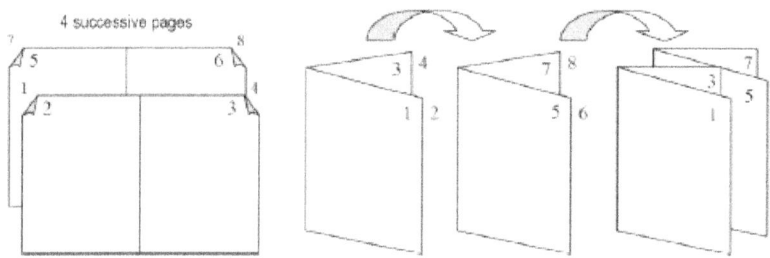

Figure 3-13 shows how this process works using an eight-page document as an example and the Sheets per booklet = 4 successive pages.

Figure 3-13. How the Sheets per booklet = 4 option influences the printing process of an 8-page document using booklet signatures of 4 pages

As you can see, when Sheets per booklet = 4 pages, each sheet of paper will receive four successive document pages. At the left side of the figure you can see that on the first printed sheet signature of four pages (front Page), the internal side of the Page will receive pages 2 and 3, while the outer side (back of Page) will receive pages 1 and 4. The second printed sheet signature will receive pages 5 and 6 (front) and 7 and 8 (back).

Since each sheet signature is composed by four successive pages, each one must be folded in the middle to compose a single notebook of four successive document pages, which will then be stacked to bring the right document page sequence to the final eight-page booklet.

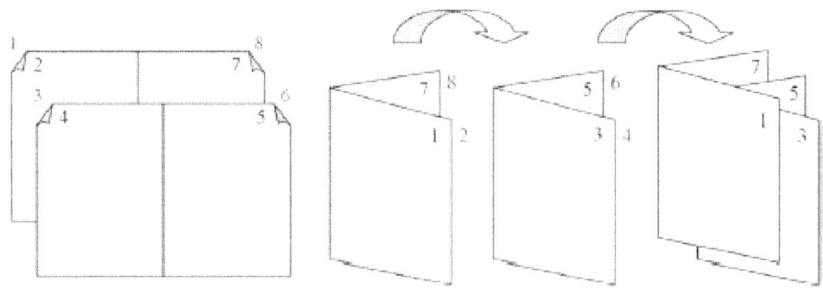

Figure 3-14 shows how this process works for the same eight-page document with Sheets per booklet = 8 successive pages.

Figure 3-14. How the Sheets per booklet = 8 option influences the printing process of an 8-page document using booklets of 4-page signatures

This time things are completely different. When Sheets per booklet = 8 pages, each sheet signature will no longer receive four successive document pages. Since it will use 8/4 = 2 sheet signatures to create each notebook; each sheet signature will

MICROSOFT WORD

receive the page numbers that will give the right page sequence when two next page signatures are stacked and folded.

At the left side of the figure you can see that on the first printed sheet signature of four pages (front Page), the internal side of the Page will receive pages 4 and 5, while the outer side (back of Page) will receive pages 3 and 6. The second printed sheet signature will receive pages 2 and 7 (front) and 1 and 8 (back). Since these two page signatures must be stacked and folded together to create a two-page notebook made up of eight successive pages that will bring the right document page sequence to the eight pages of the final booklet.

Attention: Microsoft Word uses the Sheets per Booklet = Auto = 40 pages as a maximum value, because 40/4 = 10 sheet signatures is the maximum number of pages that can be stacked and folded together without creating too much bulk.

If you have long text documents like Sense and Sensibility or The Last of the Mohicans, which have more than 150 pages (according to page size, margins, and formatting options used), and want to print them and bind them into booklets, you must set Sheets per booklet = Auto or 40, to not end up with many sheets of paper to stack and fold, which will not work for staples or even for the final document paper fold itself, unless if you plan to cut the sheet of papers in the middle using a professional paper cutter and spiral-bind them together.

Whenever you select Multiple pages = Book fold to produce a booklet, Microsoft Word will

- Change the document's page Orientation to Landscape.

- Change page width to half the original height of the paper size selected (if the original page size was Letter, 8.5 × 11, the document page will receive a width = 5.5).

- Double the number of document pages.

- Print the document as expected, but not show how the pages will be printed, either in document view or in the File➤ Print window.

So, follow these rules whenever you want to produce an appropriate booklet printing:

- Use a font size between 10 pt and 12 pt for the body text.
- Use a font size not bigger than 16 pt for chapter and section titles.
- Change page margins to half the original size.
- Set the Different Odd and Even options in the Headers and footers area of the Layout tab of the Page Setup dialog box.
- Set Sheets per booklet = All, if you plan to cut the sheet signatures in half, using a professional paper cutter.
- Set Sheets per booklet = Auto, if you plan to spiral bind the final booklet to create notebooks of up to 10 successive sheet signatures (of four pages each).
- Print the book using a PDF printer (like CutePDF) so you can store and see the final result before printing the book (the File➤ Export to PDF/XPS option will not work this time).
- Use a double-side printer for better results. If you don't have such a printer, print all the odd pages first, invert the printed stack of sheets, put them on the printer tray again (with printed side up), and print all the even pages.

MICROSOFT WORD

Formatting Tips

Open the "European Convention of Human Rights.docx" document in Microsoft Word and note that the document has 13 pages, receiving Title, Subtitle, Heading1, and Heading2 styles formatted with the Simple style set (selected from the Design tab Style Set gallery). Heading1 style was changed by checking the Paragraph▶ Page break before option, and Heading2 style was changed by checking the Paragraph▶ Keep with next option (Figure 3-15).

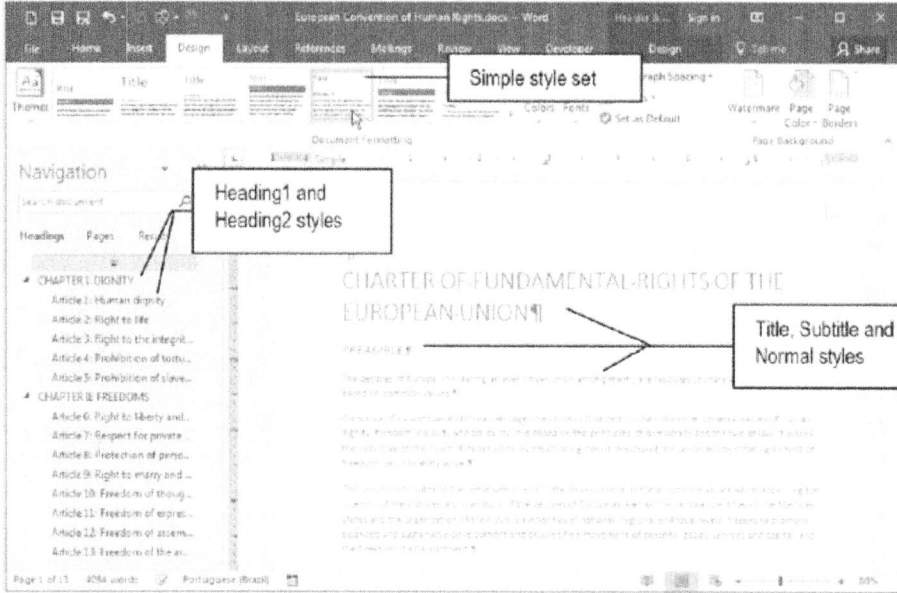

Figure 3-15. The "European Convention of Human Rights.docx" received styles Title, Subtitle, Heading1, Heading2 (see the Navigation pane), and Normal. It was formatted with the Simple style set selected in the Design tab's Style Set gallery.

Double-click the ruler to show the Page Setup dialog box, and note in the Page tab that it is formatted with a Letter size page (8.5 × 11).

MICROSOFT WORD

In the Margin tab that it has Top, Bottom, and Outside margins = 0.5 and Inside margin = 1, with Multiple Pages, = Mirror Margins (the inside margin is bigger than outside). In Layout tab note that it has Different odd and even and Different first page options checked, which gives it different first Page, odd, and even page headers (Figure 3-16).

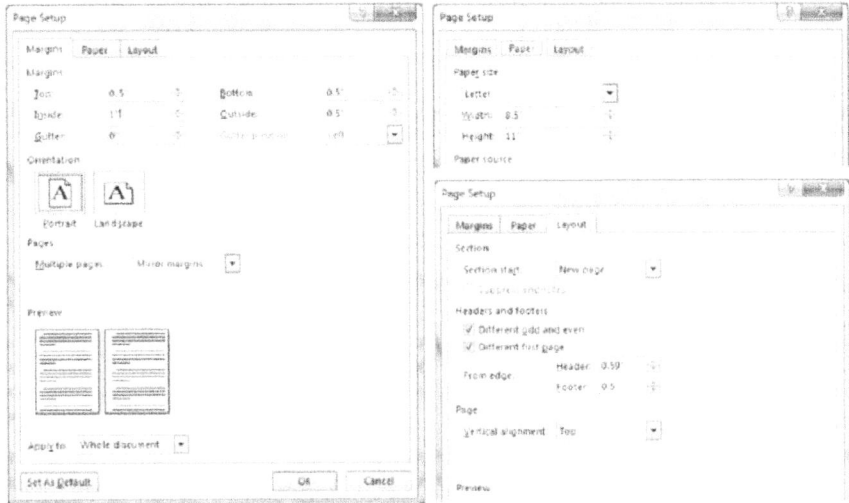

Figure 3-16. Double-click the ruler to show the Page Setup dialog box and note that the "European Convention of Human Rights.docx" document uses a Letter page, with 0.5" Top, Bottom, and Outside margins, and 1" inside margin, with Different odd and even and Different first page header options checked.

Close the Page Setup dialog box, press Page Down key to move to page 2, and note that it has a Table of Contents. Look to page 2 and 3 headers and note they received the modified Accent Bar 1 and 2 header styles (by adding the NumPages field), and that there is just one Right tab stop positioned at the inside margin of the Even Page

MICROSOFT WORD

Header and likewise at the outside margin of the Odd Page Header (right margin of both page types).

Conclusion

In this chapter, we discussed page formatting: size, orientation, margins, and header and footer areas.

You learned how to access these areas using a double-click, and how to format them using the ruler controls or the page setup dialog box. Microsoft Word offers the Header & Footer Tools Design tab full of important tools that allow creation of a different first header page, and different odd and even pages for documents that can be printed on both sides of paper.

We also talked about how to create well-formatted e-books, how to export good PDF documents (using the Table of Contents to generate the PDF BookMarks), and how to create booklets by setting the Multiple pages option to Book Fold, and the differences that may arise by selecting the Sheets per booklet options.

In the next chapter, you will learn how to Edit Text using words to make your text readable and ready for publishing. So let's go to the next Chapter. Mind you, a practice they say make perfection, so practice all you've learned so far until you attain a competent unconscious level.

CHAPTER 4

TEXT EDITION

The same commands that you use to edit text in one Microsoft Office program work almost exactly the same way in another. In Word, Excel, and PowerPoint, you click where you want the new text to go and begin typing.

The insertion point is the flashing vertical marker (cursor) that shows where the text that you type will appear. You can move the insertion point with the arrow keys, or you can click where you want to place it.

When the mouse pointer is over an area where you can place text, it turns into an I-shaped pointer called an I-beam. The shape of the I-beam makes it easy for you to precisely position it, even between two tiny characters of text.

To insert new text, position the insertion point where you want to insert it and then type the new text.

To remove text, you can use any of these methods:

Backspace it: Position the insertion point and then press the Backspace key to delete text to the left of the insertion point.

Delete it: Select the text and then press the Delete key, or position the insertion point and then press the Delete key to delete text to the right of the insertion point.

Type over it. Select the text and then type new text to replace it. Whatever was selected would be deleted.

In Word, you can't move the insertion point past the end of the document, so if you want the insertion point in the center of the document, for example, you'd normally have to press Enter to create extra blank paragraphs until it arrives where you want it. To get around that, double-click where you want the insertion point. Even if it's beyond the end of the document, it moves there (and the end of the document moves down past the new location).

Edit a Microsoft Word document

If you do not see the option to edit these files, you do not have the required SED.SU - Secure Editing of Office Documents (Word, PPT, and Excel) license. Contact your administrator if you need this feature.

1. Open the file that you want to edit.

Basic Text Editing

You can use any of the following techniques to correct errors in a document and make other desired changes, such as adding text. The techniques vary, depending on whether you are changing selected or unselected text.

To delete unselected Text:

- Position the text insertion mark immediately to the right or left of the text you want to correct or remove (Figure 4.1).

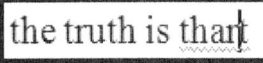

Figure 4.1 Set the text insertion mark to the right or left of the text you want to delete.

MICROSOFT WORD

- Do one of the following:

  - To delete the previous character (the one to the left), press **backspace**.

  - To delete the next character (the one to the right), press **del.** or **delete**.

To delete additional characters, continue pressing **backspace**, **del**, or **delete**.

- If necessary, replace the deleted text by typing new characters.

To delete or replace selected text:

To select text (Figure 4.2) to be deleted or replaced, do one of the following:

- Set the text insertion mark at one end of the text to be selected, and then drag to or shift and click the opposite end.

- Set the text insertion mark at one end of the text to be selected, and then while holding down shift press arrow keys to move to the end of the text.

- Double-click to select a word or triple-click to select a paragraph.

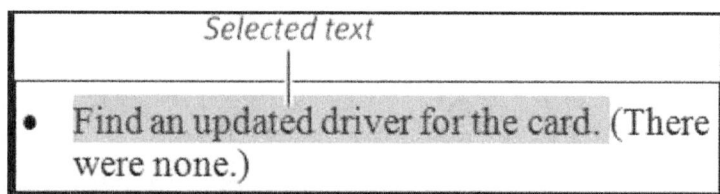

Figure 4.2 Selected text is highlighted like this.

Do one of the following:

MICROSOFT WORD

- To delete the selected text, press del.jpg, backspace.jpg, or delete.jpg.
- To replace the selected text, type the replacement text. When you begin typing, the selected text is deleted.

Selecting Partial Words

If you find that you're frequently (and automatically) selecting entire words when trying to select partial words, the reason is that a Word Options setting is getting in your way.

To change this setting, click the File tab. In the Backstage, click Options. In the Word Options dialog box, select the Advanced category and remove the check mark from **When selecting, automatically select entire word** (Figure 4.3, above). Click OK to save the new setting.

101

MICROSOFT WORD

Figure 4.3 click the File tab

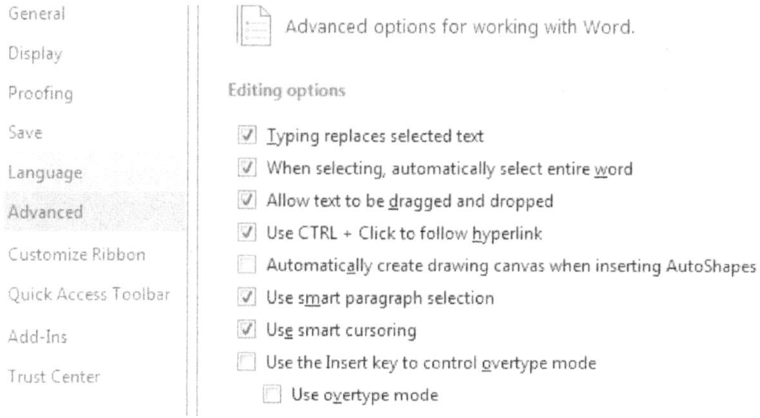

Figure 4.4 To simplify text selection, remove the check mark from the second check box in the Editing options section.

To insert new text:

- Position the text insertion mark where you want to add the new text.

You can insert new text anywhere in a document.

- Do either of the following:

- Type the new text.
- Paste the new text by clicking the Paste icon in the Clipboard group of the Home tab or by pressing ctrl-v.jpg.

HINTS

- You can also delete text by cutting it. Unlike a normal deletion, cut text is stored in the Clipboard (and the Office Clipboard), where it's available for pasting. To cut selected text, click the Cut icon in the Clipboard group of the Home tab (see Figure 4.5) or press ctrl-x.

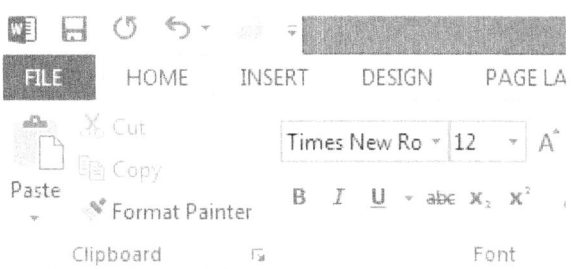

Figure 4.5 Showing the Cut icon in the Clipboard group of the Home tab

- You can use drag-and-drop to move selected text from one location to another—either within a document or between Word documents. This is equivalent to performing a cut-and-paste.

If you want a drag-and-drop to leave the original text intact (working as a copy-and-paste rather than as a cut-and-paste), drag the selected text using the right mouse button. From the context menu that appears at the destination (Figure 4.6), choose **Copy Here**.

MICROSOFT WORD

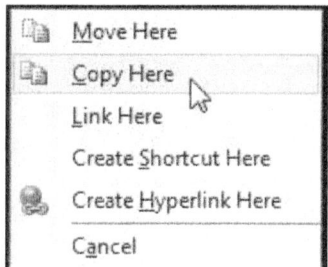

Figure 4.6 When right-dragging text, you can elect to perform a copy rather than a move.

To undo the most recent edit, immediately click the Undo icon in the Quick Access Toolbar (Figure 4.7) or press ctrl-z. (Note that you can undo multiple actions by clicking the Undo icon's down arrow.)

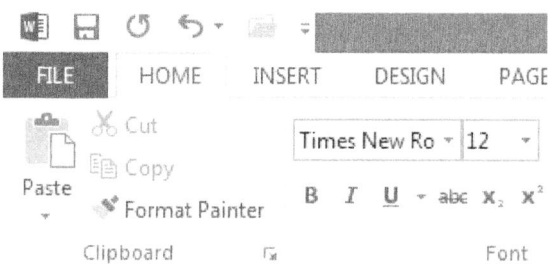

Figure 4.7 You can often reverse your most recent action.

Controlling Paste Formatting

When you paste text into a Word document, its formatting is determined by settings in the Advanced section of the Word Options dialog box. Depending on the text's source and whether the styles conflict, either the original formatting is retained or the text is reformatted to match the surrounding text at the destination. However, you can override the default Paste formatting.

When pasting, the Paste Options icon appears at the end of or beneath the pasted text. Click the icon to choose a formatting option.

Insert images

- Click the Insert tab.
- Place your cursor where you want to add an image.
- To add an image from your computer, click Image
- Choose the Image to add.

Mark up the document

If you are viewing a .docx file, you can use the following review features:

- Click the Review tab.
- Now, click Author to enter the name associated with the changes you make in the document.
- Turn on Track Changes if you want to keep track of the changes that you make to the document.
- Turn on Show Changes to see all the changes that have been made to the document.
- Click Accept to convert the currently selected tracked change to the final text.
- Click Reject to revert the currently selected tracked change to the previous text.
- Click Next to go to the next tracked change in the document.

MICROSOFT WORD

If you receive or open a document and can't make any changes, it might be Open for viewing only in Protected View. Follow these steps to edit:

- Go to File > Info.
- Select Protect document.
- Select Enable Editing.

CHAPTER 5

AUTOCORRECT, AUTOTEXT, AND AUTOFORMAT

Word tries its best to help you with the writing task. When you goof, mistakes are corrected. When it looks like you meant to type a special character, Word inserts the proper character for you. Formatted lists and paragraphs can also appear automatically. Some of these features save a lot of time, and some you may find get in your way. Together, these tools form what **I call the Autos**.

Know Your Autos

As you can infer from the chapter's title, Microsoft Word hosts several features that use the name Auto. They're all automatic, they serve comparable functions, and they have annoyingly similar names. Here's the Big Picture:

AutoCorrect: This function corrects common typos and capitalizations. It also inherited many of the old AutoText features from previous versions of Word.

AutoText Building Blocks: This function lets you insert preset chunks of text. It's not the same as the old AutoText feature.

AutoFormat: This feature lets you format your document in one operation. It's a holdover from earlier versions of Word. The AutoFormat command isn't even found on the Ribbon. I listed it here because it's easily confused with the AutoFormat As You Type command.

AutoFormat As You Type: This function deals with formatting text, applying similar paragraph styles (bullets, numbers, and so on), and converting individual characters to their proper equivalents (such as ½ for 1/2).

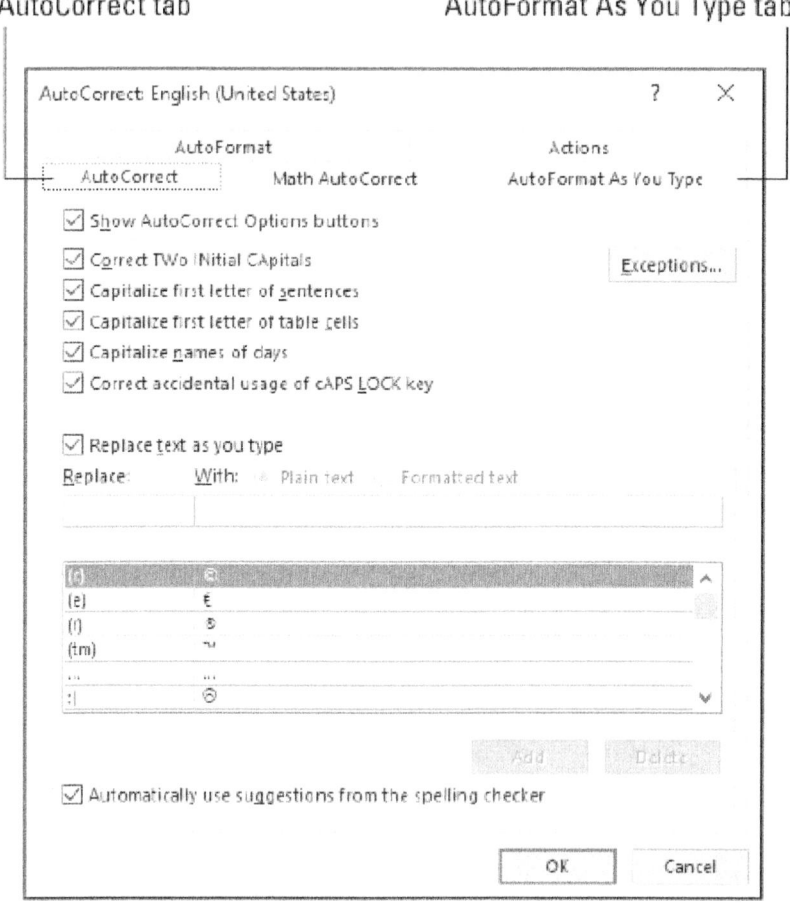

To activate the AutoCorrect dialog box, shown in Figure 5-1, follow these steps:

1. Click the File tab.

2. Choose Options.

The Word Options dialog box appears.

3. Choose Proofing from the left side of the Word Options dialog box.

4. By the right side of the dialog box, click the AutoCorrect Options button. Behold the AutoCorrect dialog box.

AutoCorrect the Boo-Boos

Word's AutoCorrect feature supplements the spell check proofing tool. Basically, AutoCorrect lets you avoid the shame of having to proof certain words in your text. When AutoCorrect is active, common typos and capitalization errors are corrected automatically.

Working with AutoCorrect capitalization settings

It's not that you don't know how or when to capitalize words. No, the problem is that sneaky Shift key. When you're too late or too early with that key, or you dawdle too long, you create capitalization typos. The word may be flagged as misspelled, though it's just the uppercase/lowercase letters that are different.

The common capitalization errors are illustrated in Figure 5-2, which is a closeup of part of the AutoCorrect dialog box (the AutoCorrect tab). These five settings cover the most common Shift key boo-boos.

AutoFormat	Actions
AutoCorrect Math AutoCorrect	AutoFormat As You Type

☑ Show AutoCorrect Options buttons
☑ Correct TWo INitial CApitals   [Exceptions...]
☑ Capitalize first letter of sentences
☑ Capitalize first letter of table cells
☑ Capitalize names of days
☑ Correct accidental usage of cAPS LOCK key

To turn one or more of the capitalization settings on or off, obey these directions:

1. Click the File tab and choose Options.
2. Choose Proofing on the left side of the Word Options dialog box.
3. Click the AutoCorrect Options button.
4. Ensure that the AutoCorrect tab is selected.
5. Remove or add check marks by the options you want to deactivate or activate, respectively.

For example, if you don't want the first letter of a sentence capitalized in your poetry, remove the check mark by the option Capitalize First Letter of Sentences.

6. Click the OK button when you're done, and click OK again to close the Word Options dialog box.

Click the Exceptions button (refer to Figure 5-2) to direct AutoCorrect not to capitalize certain words. For example, AutoCorrect doesn't interpret the period after a common abbreviation at the end of a sentence. That's because those abbreviations are listed in the AutoCorrect Exceptions dialog box, shown in Figure 5-3.

MICROSOFT WORD

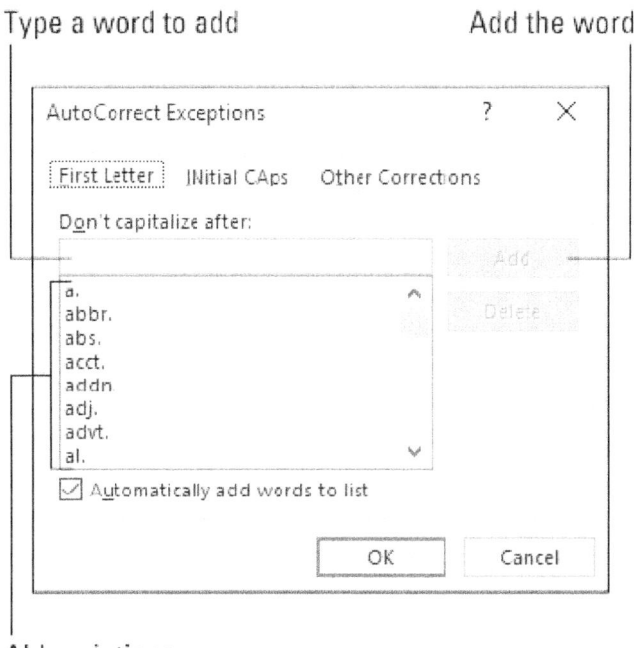

Abbreviations

You can add your own abbreviations to the list: Type the text into the box (refer to Figure 5-3) and click the Add button.

The **INitial CAps** tab lets you set exceptions for proper words that require more than one initial capital letter. Click the tab to see one example: IDs, short for identifications.

The Other Corrections tab allows you to type any old jumble of lowercase and capital letters and add each word to a list. AutoCorrect then ignores those words. My advice is to create this list as you work on your document. If the capitalization IdaHO is required in your text, add that exact word as an exception in the Auto- Correct Exceptions dialog box.

Pretending that AutoCorrect is AutoText

AutoCorrect's second feature (after fixing capitalization errors) is replacing common typos and other text with correct versions. This feature is similar to the old AutoText feature and is endeared by Word users from generation's past.

The first set of corrections converts common text abbreviations into their appropriate symbols, such as (C) into the copyright symbol, ©. These symbols are located at the top of the list of Replace Text As You Type list, illustrated in Figure 5-4 (top).

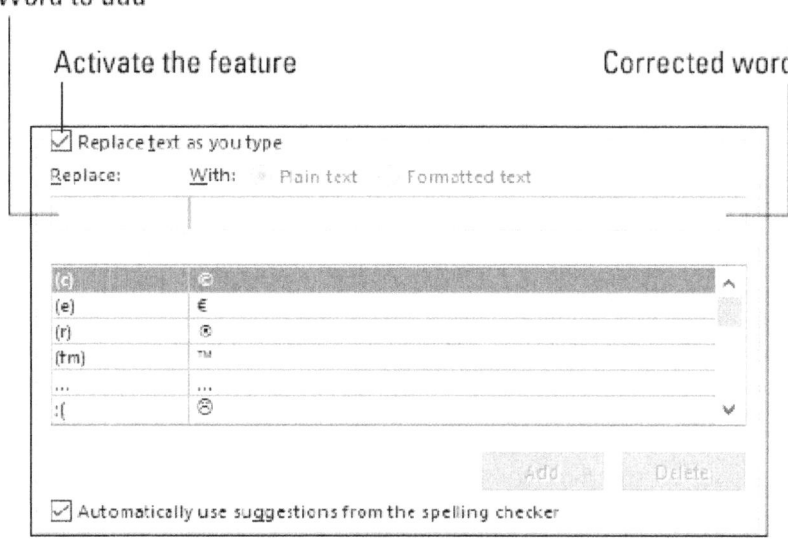

Symbols

MICROSOFT WORD

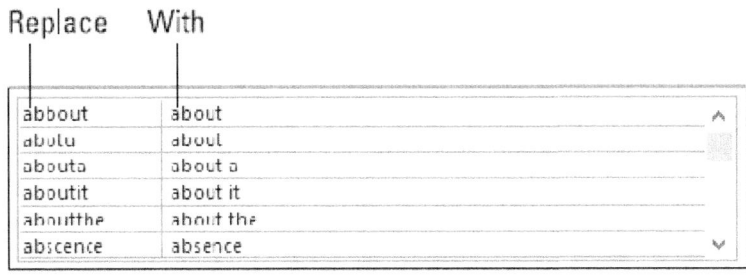

Text typos

Beyond symbols, AutoCorrect's replace-text list includes common typos, shown at the bottom in Figure 5-4. When you type one of the items on the left side of the list, Word automatically inserts the proper text on the right providing that the Replace Text As You Type command is active.

To ensure that the feature is active, or to add another word to correct, obey these steps:

1. Click the File tab and choose Options.
2. In the Word Options dialog box, choose Proofing on the left side.
3. Click the AutoCorrect Options button.

The AutoCorrect dialog box appears with the AutoCorrect tab up front.

4. Ensure that there's a check mark by the option **Replace Text As You Type**.

When the check mark is present, the feature is active.

To add another word, such as break to replace braek, continue with Step 5.

5. In the Replace text box, type the word you frequently mistype. For example, break;
6. In the box, type the word to replace the mistyped word. Such as break.
7. Click the Add button.

MICROSOFT WORD

8. Click OK to close the AutoCorrect dialog box, and then OK to close the Word Options dialog box.

You can repeat Steps 5 through 7 to add a number of your favorite typos. Whenever the word you specify in Step 5 is typed, the word you enter for Step 6 replaces it automatically.

Undoing an AutoCorrect change

Every time AutoCorrect fixes capitalization, it inserts a proper symbol, or corrects a typo, and a small symbol appears in the document's text. You may not see it, so point the mouse at any word that is changed by AutoCorrect. Upon success, a small, blue rectangle appears in the text.

Point the mouse at the rectangle to see the AutoCorrect Options. Click the button to reveal a menu, which allows you to do one of three things:

Undo: Choose the Change Back command to revert the change. You see the original word or characters listed in the menu.

Stop correcting: Choose the Stop Automatically Correcting command to remove the word from the AutoCorrect list. If you select this command, the selected word will never be corrected again, not in any document.

View the AutoCorrect dialog box: Choose the bottom command on the menu to visit the AutoCorrect dialog box, and the AutoCorrect tab.

If you find yourself becoming annoyed with all the automatic corrections, disable the AutoCorrect Replace As You Type feature. Consider these directions:

1. Click the File tab and choose Options.

2. Choose Proofing, and then click the AutoCorrect Options button.
3. In the AutoCorrect dialog box, on the AutoCorrect tab, remove the check mark by the item **Replace As You Type**.
4. Click OK to close the AutoCorrect dialog box.
5. Click OK to close the Word Options dialog box.

If you merely want to disable the AutoCorrect Options button, follow Steps 1 and 2, but in Step 3 remove the check mark by the option Show AutoCorrect Options Buttons.

AutoFormat As You Type

Word's AutoFormat feature automatically applies character formats and paragraph styles to your text. It works similarly to AutoCorrect, in that AutoFormat makes its changes on the fly. But of the two features, AutoFormat causes users more woe. It tends to make assumptions you may not agree with. That's okay! You can cheerfully disable the feature.

Understanding AutoFormat options

The AutoFormat function hosts a suite of routines, some of which might fall under the category of AutoCorrect, but geniuses at Microsoft placed them under Auto-Format instead. The AutoFormat routines include

Replace As You Type: This feature converts some characters and text sequences into other characters, such as -- (two hyphens) into an — (em dash), or 1/2 into ½. Word also creates hyperlinks for web page addresses and network paths.

Apply As You Type: This feature converts text into formatted elements, including bulleted lists, numbered lists, tables, and so on. This is the AutoFormat feature most people find annoying.

Automatically As You Type: This feature copies special paragraph formatting to subsequent paragraphs, such as when you set paragraph indents or create a hanging indent list.

A summary of specific options for these features appears at the end of this section.

Okay to ignore this tab — AutoFormat tab

AutoFormat As You Type tab

AutoCorrect dialog:

AutoCorrect | Math AutoCorrect | AutoFormat | Actions | AutoFormat As You Type

Replace as you type
- ☑ 'Straight quotes' with 'smart quotes'
- ☑ Fractions (1/2) with fraction character (½)
- ☐ *Bold* and _italic_ with real formatting
- ☑ Internet and network paths with hyperlinks
- ☑ Ordinals (1st) with superscript
- ☑ Hyphens (--) with dash (—)

Apply as you type
- ☑ Automatic bulleted lists
- ☑ Border lines
- ☐ Built-in Heading styles
- ☑ Automatic numbered lists
- ☑ Tables

Automatically as you type
- ☑ Format beginning of list item like the one before it
- ☑ Set left- and first-indent with tabs and backspaces
- ☐ Define styles based on your formatting

OK | Cancel

MICROSOFT WORD

The AutoCorrect dialog box, on the AutoFormat As You Type tab, lists all the specifics for each of these categories, as illustrated in Figure 5-5.

Follow these steps:

1. Click the File tab and choose Options.
2. Choose Proofing on the left side of the Word Options dialog box.
3. On the right side of the dialog box, click the AutoCorrect Options button.
4. Click the AutoFormat As You Type tab.

Don't click the AutoFormat tab. It shows similar items, but they apply to the all-at-once AutoFormat command.

To display the AutoCorrect dialog box, and the AutoFormat As You Type tab, the actions listed in the dialog box affect text as you type. If something annoys you, which is frequently the case, you can undo the action or disable the feature. See the next section.

Undoing an AutoFormat Change

The AutoFormat command can be subtle, such as when straight quotes are converted to curly quotes, or it can be overt, such as when an automatic numbered list is created for you.

For AutoFormat's Replace As You Type features, undoing a conversion works similarly to undoing an AutoCorrect change: See the earlier section "Undoing an AutoCorrect change."

For more major text adjustments, you see the AutoFormat Options button, illustrated in Figure 5-6.

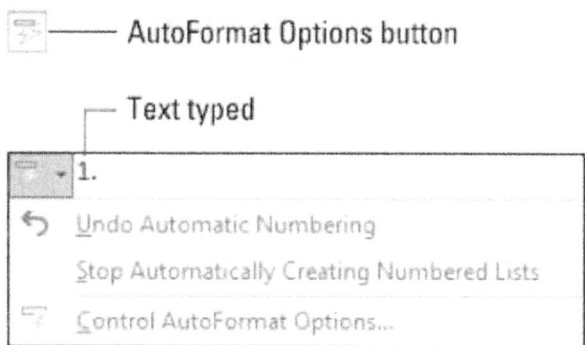

As an example, when you type 1. and then a tab, AutoFormat converts the line into a numbered paragraph, complete with indents. To undo that action, immediately follow these steps:

1. Click the AutoFormat Options button.
2. Choose the Undo Automatic Numbering command.

You can also press Esc, but you must be quick.

If you detest automatic paragraph numbering, choose the option Stop Automatically Creating Numbered Lists and that command directly dispenses with the feature.

CHAPTER 6

FORMATING TABLES

Inserting Tables

Microsoft Word tables are the modern way to tabulate text (tab stops were the typewriter way, and even today, tab stops have their place). Although there is more than one way to create a table (you can use Tab stops), it might be better to create it using the intuitive Table control found in the Illustrations area of the Insert tab of the Ribbon, which drops down a visual tool from where you can select the size of the table to be created: see the cursor's position in Figure 7-1.

MICROSOFT WORD

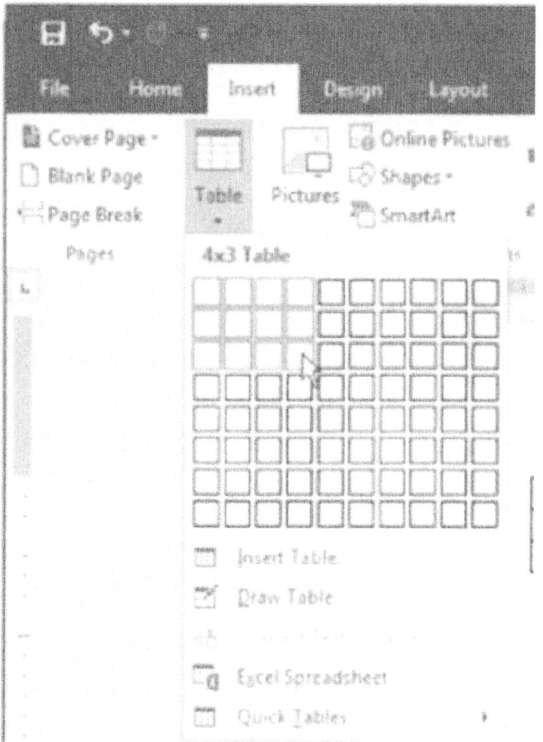

Figure 7-1. To insert a new table in the document, use the Insert tab Table command to define the number of rows and columns that the table must have. This figure draws a 3-row-by-4-column table. Click the mouse to finish the operation.

Figure 7-1 created a 3×4 table (12 cells) on the document page. Note that each cell of the figure shows the "¤" hidden character, which defines where the cell text ends, because the Show/Hide command found in the Paragraph area of the Home tab of the Ribbon is checked.

Each table cell can hold any amount of text, and you can navigate through its cells by directly clicking it with the mouse, or using the

Tab key: each time the Tab key is pressed, Word moves to the next cell.

Attention *To insert another table row, click the last table cell and press the Tab key. Inheritance will take care to copy the current row format to the new table row.*

Typing Text in Table Cells

You can consider Microsoft Word table cells as mini documents where you can insert and format paragraphs like you do in any other document area. You can press Enter and insert one or more paragraphs in any cell, or press Ctrl+Enter to insert a Line break, or even press Ctrl+Tab to insert one or more Tab characters inside a single cell. And for each of these paragraphs, you can define all available formatting options (alignment, indentation, line space, space before and after).

Now, with all the knowledge you have gathered so far in this book, think about the mess we can create in a single cell if we are not aware of such hidden characters.

Figure 7-2 shows what happened to the first table cell after you insert a Tab, a Shift+Enter (Line break), and the two Enter keys changed the alignment of its last paragraph.

Note that all other cells in the same row now have the same height. The figure shows the same table with the Show/Hide option checked and unchecked so you can draw your own conclusions!

MICROSOFT WORD

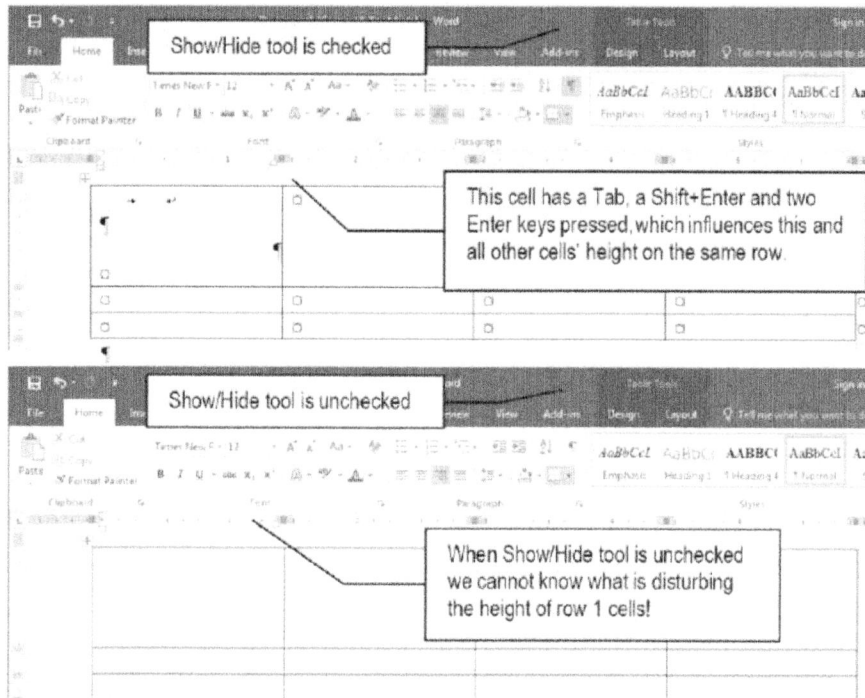

Figure 7-2. Consider Microsoft Word table cells as mini documents where you can insert paragraphs and hidden characters. This figure shows a cell with hidden characters inserted, which changed the height of that cell, affecting all other cells of the same row. Without the Show/Hide tool checked, one cannot anticipate what will happen to a table that gets such a high height row.

And this is not all, Microsoft Tables are so versatile that you can also insert another table inside any of its cells. Figure 7-3 shows two tables: the first one is the same table used by Figure 7-1 that now has tables inserted inside two of its cells (cells (1,2) and (2,3)—the first number index describe the row number and the second the column number), while the second table is a more common problem: a one-cell table (external, which has two Enter keys so you can see it better) that received another table inside it.

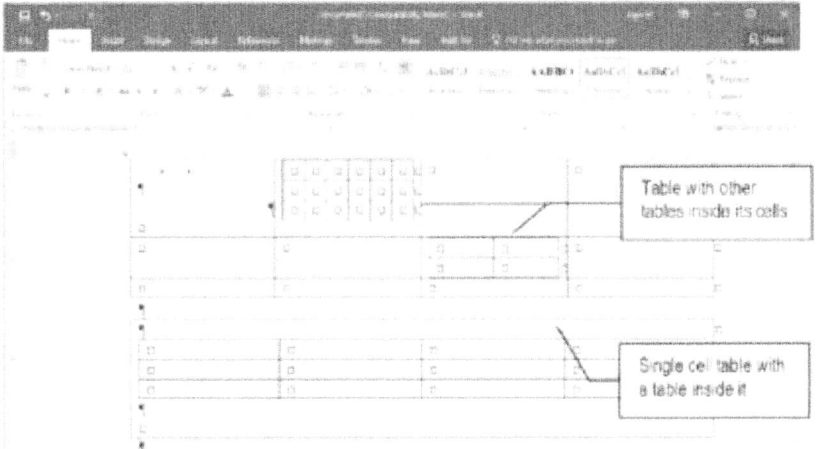

Figure 7-3. This figure shows two different tables, both having tables inserted inside table cells. The second case shows a single-cell table with a table inserted inside it.

Convert Table to Text and Vice Versa

You should understand that once a table exists in the document; you can always convert it to text (and conversely convert any text to table).

This double-conversion process may sometimes be the only way to correctly re-create a table.

To convert any table to text, follow these steps:
- Click anywhere inside the table to select it (or click the "+" square in the top left table corner to select the entire table);

- In the Table Tools ➤ Layout tab that appears on Ribbon whenever a table is selected, click the Convert to Text command;

- Microsoft Word will show the Convert Table to Text dialog box, asking how you want to separate the table values;

- Choose the separator character to be used as cell content delimiter and press Enter to finish the conversation process.

Figure 7-4 shows what happens when we convert to text an empty 5×4 table using Tab stops as cell separator. Note that Word inserts n-1 tab stops to delimit each table cell value (where n = the table columns count), using a pilcrow paragraph mark to separate each table row.

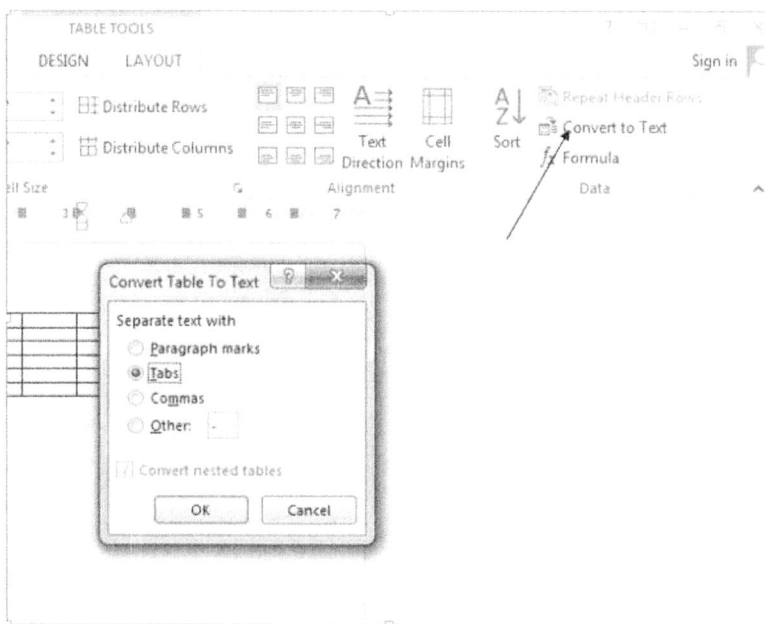

Figure 7-4. You can convert any table to text selecting the table and using the Table Tools ➤ Layout tab ➤ Convert to Text

command. Microsoft Word will ask to select the cell separator character that must be used to separate each cell content (default is Tab).

You are now in a position to appreciate the need to understand what a Tab character means. Looking to Figure 7-4, you must understand that no text was inserted in the Table, the three tab stops of these five paragraphs can represent a 5×4 table (with the first cell content being at left of the first Tab character)!

To reconvert the selected text to a table, follow these steps:

- Select just the text paragraphs that you want to convert to a table (no less, no more);

- In the Insert tab of the Ribbon, click the Table ➤ Convert Text to Table command;

- Microsoft Word will show the Convert Text to Table dialog box, guessing the table dimensions and cell separator character it will consider to create the table, relative to the text you selected;

- If everything is OK, press Enter to convert the text to a table.

Figure 7-5 shows how easy it was to reconvert the perfect 5×4 table, which was previously converted to text, using Tab stops as cell character separator.

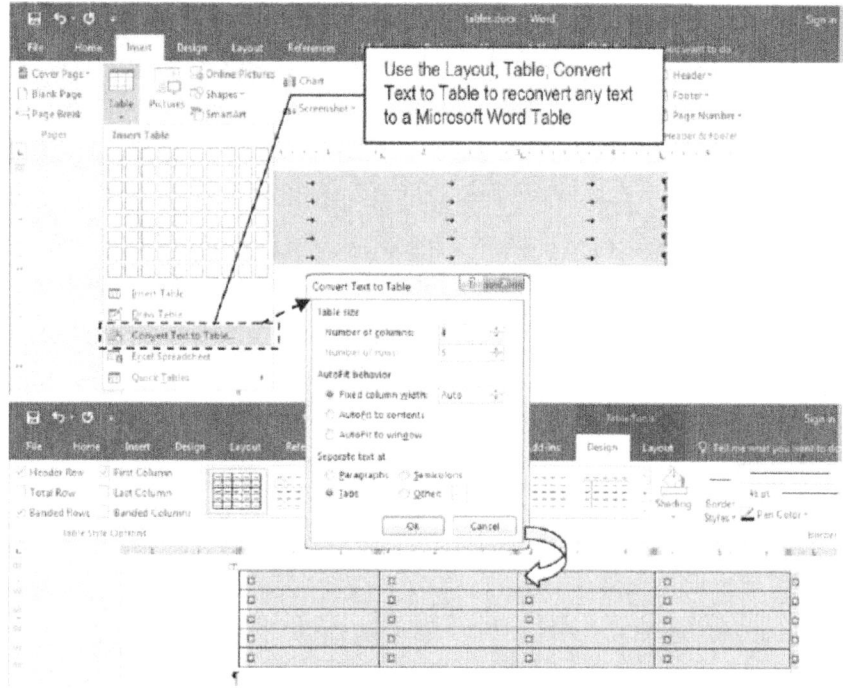

Figure 7-5. To convert text to table, select just the paragraphs you want to convert (no more, no less), click the Insert tab on the Ribbon, and apply the Table ➤ Convert Text to Table command. Microsoft Word will show the Convert Text to Table dialog box, making a guess of which type of table it can create based on the selected text.

But if the table is too complex like the ones shown in Figure 7-3, where a cell has a table inserted in it, the conversion of table to text may create paragraphs with very different quantities of Tab characters (or any other text separator character chosen, Figure 7-6), so that it may become impossible to reconstruct the original table design using the Table ➤ Convert Text to Table command (Figure 7-7).

MICROSOFT WORD

Attention If you have a table inserted in another table cell and want to convert it to text inside the cell, select just the inserted table before applying the Layout ➤Convert to text command.

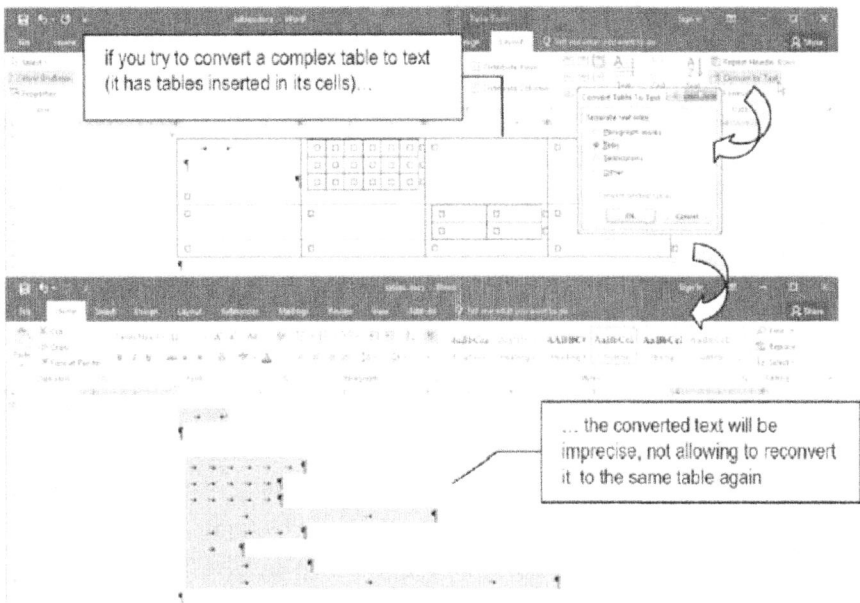

Figure 7-6. Complex table designs may create very uneven text paragraphs, having different numbers of Tab stops (or any other text separator character used by the Convert Table to Text dialog box).

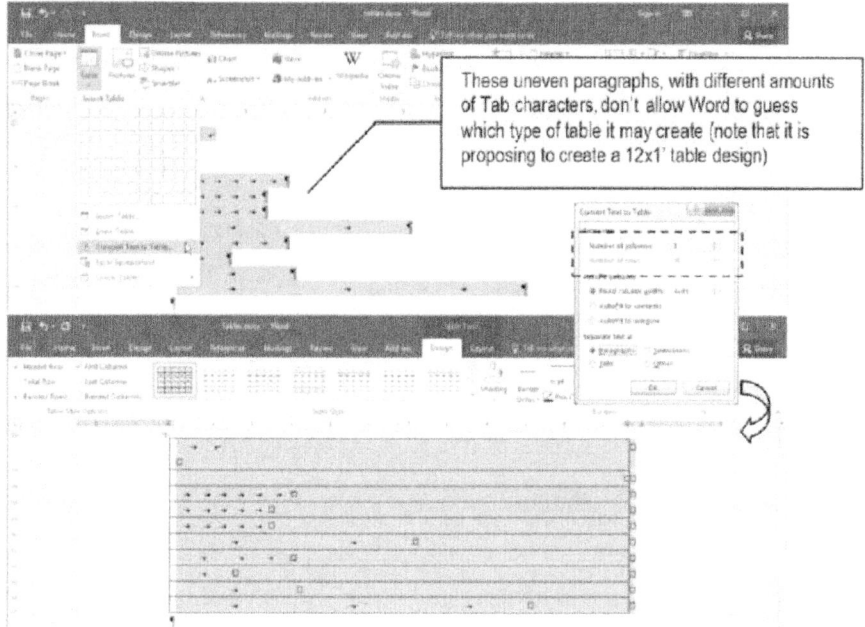

Figure 7-7. When you try to reconvert uneven paragraphs to a table, the Convert Text to Table dialog box may not be capable of "guessing" which type of table you want to create, and the result may be a table quite different from the one that generated that type of text.

Selecting and Deleting Tables and Cells

Once a table is inserted in any Microsoft Word document, it is not obvious how to delete it: it is very persistent in the document, neglecting to react to the so-obvious Delete key.

There are many strategies to delete a table from the document, using the mouse or the keyboard.

To delete a table using the mouse, you can follow these next steps:

MICROSOFT WORD

- Right-click any table cell, which makes a small floating toolbar appear above it.
- In the floating tool bar, click Delete and select Delete table.

Or use another method:
- Click any table cell.
- Click the small square at the top left table corner (the one with a "+" character) to select all table cells.
- Right-click any selected table cell, and in the pop-up menu that appears, choose Delete table (Figure 7-8).

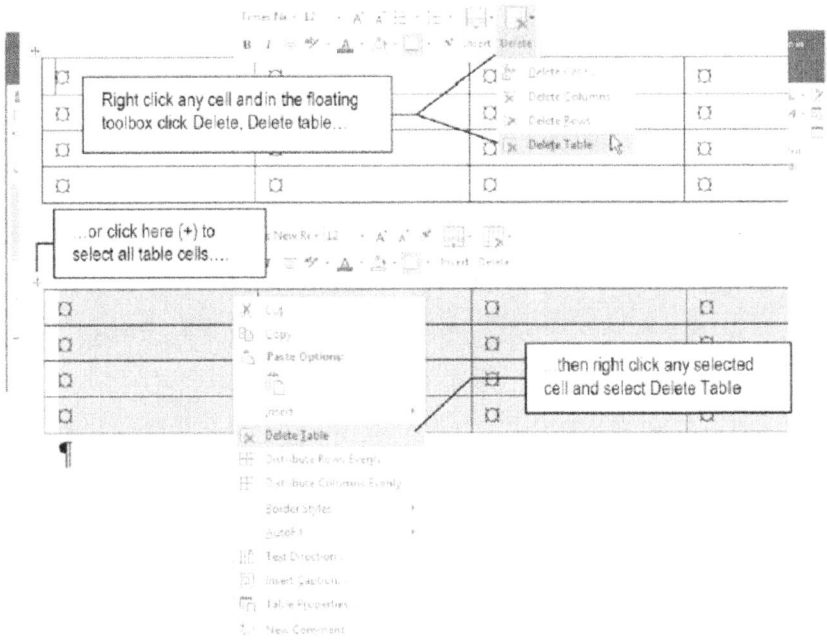

Figure 7-8. To delete a table using the mouse, right-click any of

MICROSOFT WORD

its cells and select the Delete ► Delete Table command in the small toolbox that appears. Or you can click the small box with a "+" character in the top left table corner to first select the entire table, right-click any selected cell, and select Delete Table in the pop-up menu.

To delete a table using the keyboard, you can

1. Insert one empty paragraph after the table;
2. Select the table and this empty paragraph;
3. Press Delete key.

Selecting All Table Cells to Delete a Table

Another way to delete a table from any document is by first selecting all table cells and then using Shift+Delete.

Once again, you can select all table cells by using different strategies:

- Click the first table cell and drag the mouse to select all its cells;
- Click the first table cell, press and hold Shift, and click the last table cell;
- Click any table cell and then click the small square in the small box at the top left table corner (the one with a "+" character);
- Alt+Double-click at the left of any table row (point the mouse cursor to the left of any table row until it

MICROSOFT WORD

becomes a normal mouse pointer before performing the operation).

Once the table is selected, you can quickly delete it by pressing Shift+Delete (or eventually convert the table to text and delete the associated text).

Try for yourself!

Selecting a Single Cell

Use the mouse to select any amount of contiguous table cells and apply a desired format to them:

To select a single cell, anywhere in the table;

- Point the mouse to the left of any cell (inside it) until the cursor turns into a small black arrow pointing up (indicating that just one cell will be selected);

- Click to select this cell (Figure 7-9).

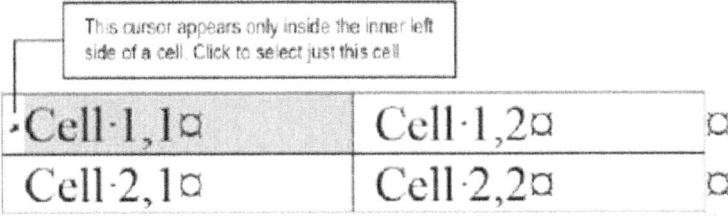

Figure 7-9. Point the mouse inside any cell's inner left side until it changes to a small black arrow and click to select it

MICROSOFT WORD

Selecting Table Rows and Columns

You can select an entire row or column by dragging the mouse or using the right mouse cursor for the task.

To select a row or column by dragging the mouse:

- Click first cell row/column cell.
- Drag the mouse to left (or down) to select the entire row (or column).

To select an entire row using the mouse cursor:

- Point the mouse to the left of any row (outside the table) until the cursor changes to a regular mouse arrow.
- Click to select the entire row (Figure 7-10).

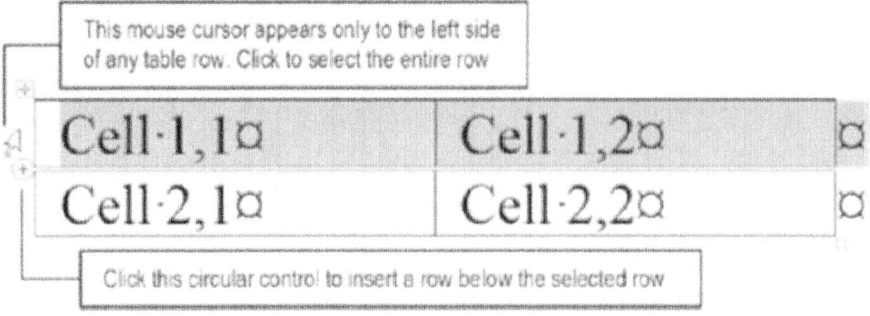

Figure 7-10. Point the mouse to the left of the first table column until it changes to a normal mouse arrow and click to select the

entire row. Displace it toward the bottom of the row to show the "add row" circular control and click to insert a new row below it.

Inserting Table Rows, Columns, and Cells

You can insert rows, columns, and cells in any Microsoft Word table by using different methods using the mouse and menu commands. Let's see them!

Using the Mouse with Table Handles

As Figures 7-10 explain, you can easily insert a new row or column in a table by selecting the desired row(s) or column(s), displacing the mouse to point to the bottom of the last row selected (or to the right of the last column border) to show the circular control with a "+" character, and clicking it.

The row(s) (or column(s)) will be inserted below (or to the right of) the last row (or column) that is selected (Figure 7-11).

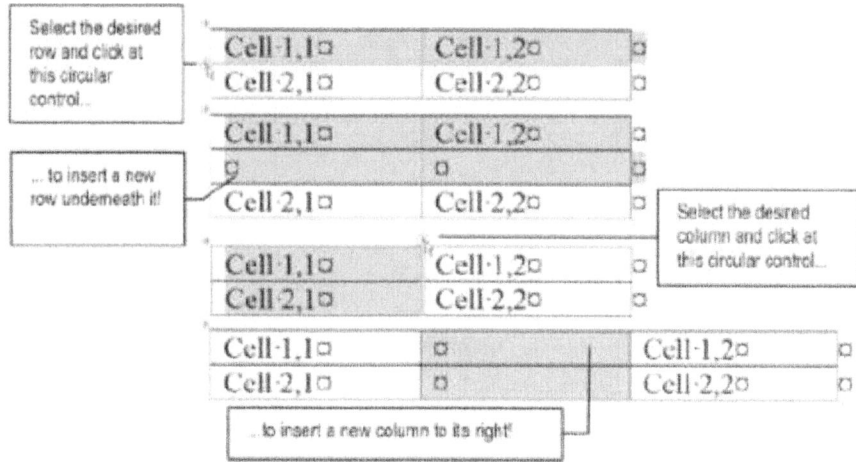

Figure 7-11. Click the circular control (with the "+" character) that appears whenever you select one or more entire rows (or columns) and point to the bottom left (or top right) of the selection, to easily insert rows at the bottom (or columns to the right) of selection.

<u>Attention</u> The number of rows or columns selected is equal to the number of rows or columns inserted.

Using Table ➤ Insert Command

Microsoft Word will also insert new cells to left or right of the current cell, allowing you to create tables that have different numbers of columns among its rows.

To insert a new cell in any table:
- Right-click the cell that will be neighbor to the cell to be inserted and choose Insert ➤ Insert cells to show the Insert Cells dialog box;

MICROSOFT WORD

- In the Insert cells dialog box, select Shift cells left or Shift cells right option to insert a single cell;

- Choose Insert entire row to insert a row below (or Insert entire column to insert a column to the right);

- Press OK to make the desired insertion.

Figure 7-12 shows how you can insert a cell to the left of a given cell using the Shift cells' right option to create a table with an uneven number of columns.

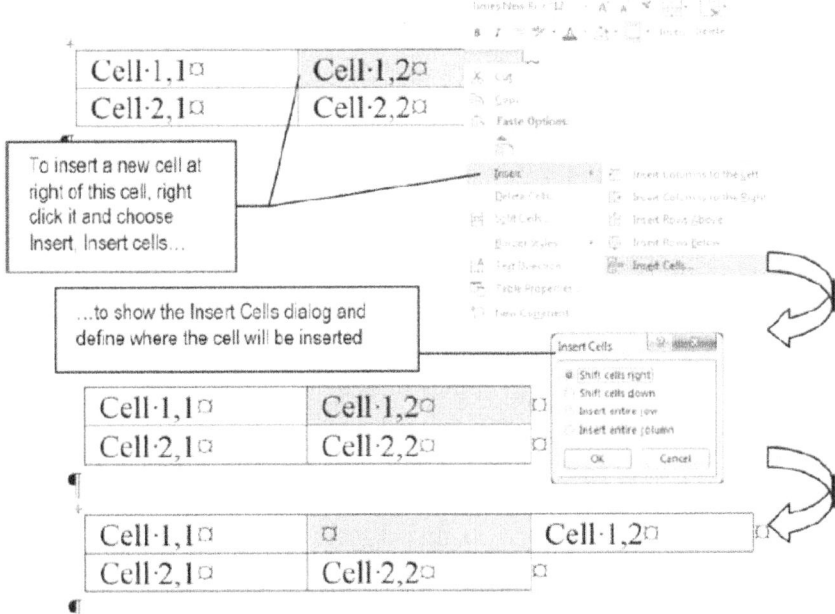

Figure 7-12. Right-click any cell and select Insert ▶ Insert cells to insert a cell to the left or right of the selected cell (you can also insert a row above or a column to the left of it).

Merging Cells

You can also create tables having rows with different column counts by merging one or more of its cells into a single cell.

To merge table cells:

- Select the cells you want to merge;
- Right-click the selection and choose Merge cells.

If the merged cells had text inside them, the text of each cell will be separated by hidden paragraph characters, with each cell using text rows inside the merged cell.

MICROSOFT WORD

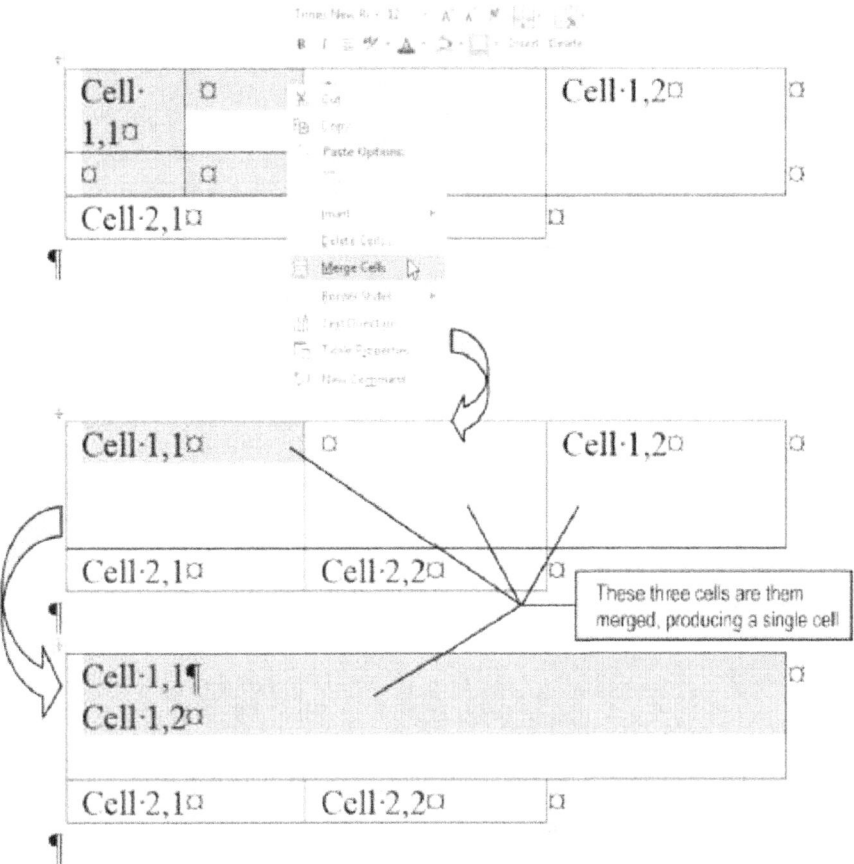

Figure 7-13. merges the four cells produced in split cell 1,1 into a single cell again. It then merges all remaining row 1 cells and merges them again into one single cell again, creating a single, big cell in row 1 with two rows of text.

Figure 7-13. Use the Merge command to join individual cells into one. If these cells have some text, the text will be separated by hidden paragraph characters inside the merged cell.

Changing Cell, Column, or Row Dimensions

Once a table has been inserted in a Microsoft Word document page, you can use the mouse to change any individual cell, column, or row dimensions, independently or at once.

Follow these simple rules:

- To change any cell width or height you must first select the desired cell. The width of all other cells in the same column will not be affected, but the height of all cells of the same row will be.

- To change any column width, you must select the entire column or no cell at all.

- Whenever you change any cell width, the entire row width will be changed.

Deleting Table Cells, Rows, and Columns

You can also delete a single cell, an entire row, or an entire column from a table. Note however that by deleting a single table you will create a hole in the table, which will oblige Microsoft Word to make a decision about what to do with the remaining cells of the row or column to which it belongs: shift all cells at its right to the left, or shift all cells at its bottom upward.

To delete a single cell, follow these steps:

- Select the cell to be deleted (point the mouse to the cell's inner left and click).

- In the small context toolbar that appears, click Delete ➤ Delete Cells to show the Delete Cells dialog box.

- Select the method that Microsoft Word must use to treat the remaining cells at its left or below (if any):

- **Shift cells left: all cells at the left of the selected cell will be displaced to the left (leaving an hole at the right of the cell row).**

- **Shift cells up: all cells below the selected cell will be displaced up.**

Figure 7-14. shows an example of what happens when you delete a single cell and select either Shift Cells Right or Shift Cells Up.

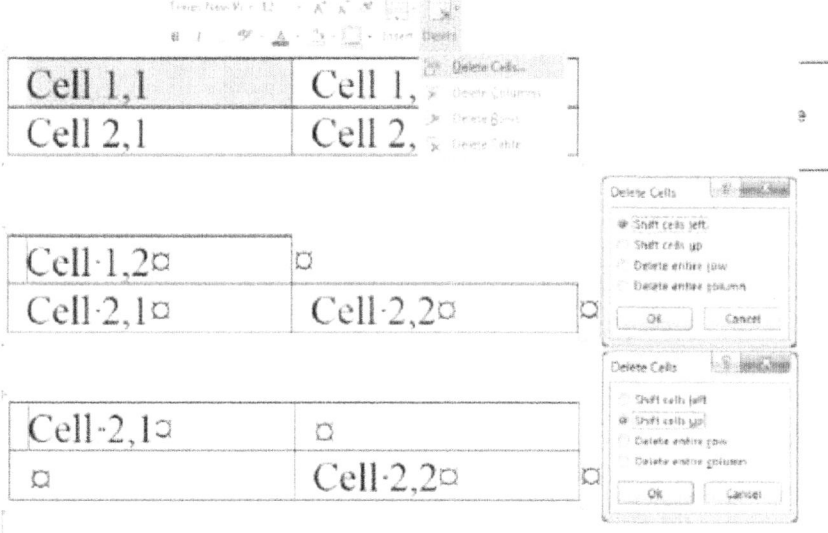

Figure 7-14. To delete a single cell or an entire row or column, select the cell first and right-click it to show the small tool bar from where you can click Delete ►Delete cells command to show the Delete Cells dialog box; once that has been done, you can take the desired action.

To delete an entire row or column from a table, you can use one of these methods:

- Select any cell from the row/column to be deleted.
- Use the Delete ➤ Delete cell command to show the Delete Cells dialog box.
- Select either Delete entire row or Delete entire column to proceed.

You can also use a faster method:

- Select the entire row or column (point the mouse over the column or at left of the row and click).
- Right-click the selection and choose Delete Row or Delete Column options (according to selection).

Table Alignment and Position

Every Microsoft Word table can be inserted as a text object in its own paragraph, or float
above the page with text paragraphs flowing around it.
This versatile way of positioning tables on the page is indeed one of the biggest sources of difficulties that you might face with table formatting. Because you did not imagine that it could be done, so you might keep fighting with the document page flow.

To see how a table is inserted on the page:

- **Right-click the table and select Table Properties in the context menu (Figure 7-15).**

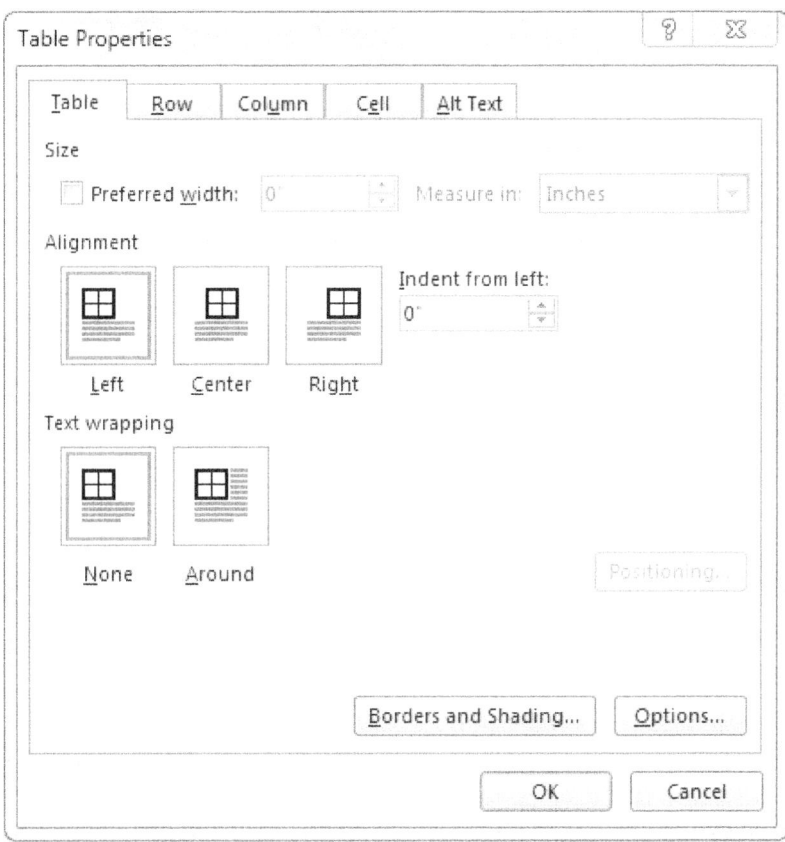

Figure 7-15. Right-click a table and select Table Properties to show the Table Properties dialog box from where you can use Text Wrapping to define that the table is a text object (None) or floats over the page (Around).

- Use the Text wrapping area to define the table behavior regarding how the text wraps around it:

- None: the table is inserted as a text element having it own paragraph.

- Around: the table is floating over the document page, with text flowing around it.

- Use the Alignment command to define the table position on the page (Left, Center, or Right aligned).

Note in the Table Properties dialog box that the Alignment option has an Indent from left option that is only enabled when Alignment = Left and Text wrapping = None, to allow defining of the table distance from the page left margin.

Use these tips to better control a table inserted in your document:
- Use Text wrapping = None to make the table to be inserted as a text element so you can better control the text that is above and below it.

- Click the small square at the top left table corner (the one with a "+" character) and drag the mouse to displace the table from the page's left margin (changing the Indent from left option of the Table Properties dialog box).

- In giving a standard cell size to all or some table cells (row height and/ or column width), select all desired table cells first and then use the other Table Properties dialog box tab controls.

Changing Table Row Size

It is not uncommon to find tables with different row heights—a formatting change that can be defined either by dragging any table row bottom border, or by inserting and removing Paragraph or Manual Line Breaks in some of its cells.

Whenever this happens, you need to check for two different options that can affect any table row height:

- Paragraph formatting options: select the entire table and check if all its cells have the same Line Spacing and Space Before and After options.

- The row height increase, and defined in the Table Properties Row tab.

The Table Properties Row tab offers special controls that allow changing all selected rows' height at once and the way a table will behave whenever it's big enough to fit on a single page (Figure 10-16).

MICROSOFT WORD

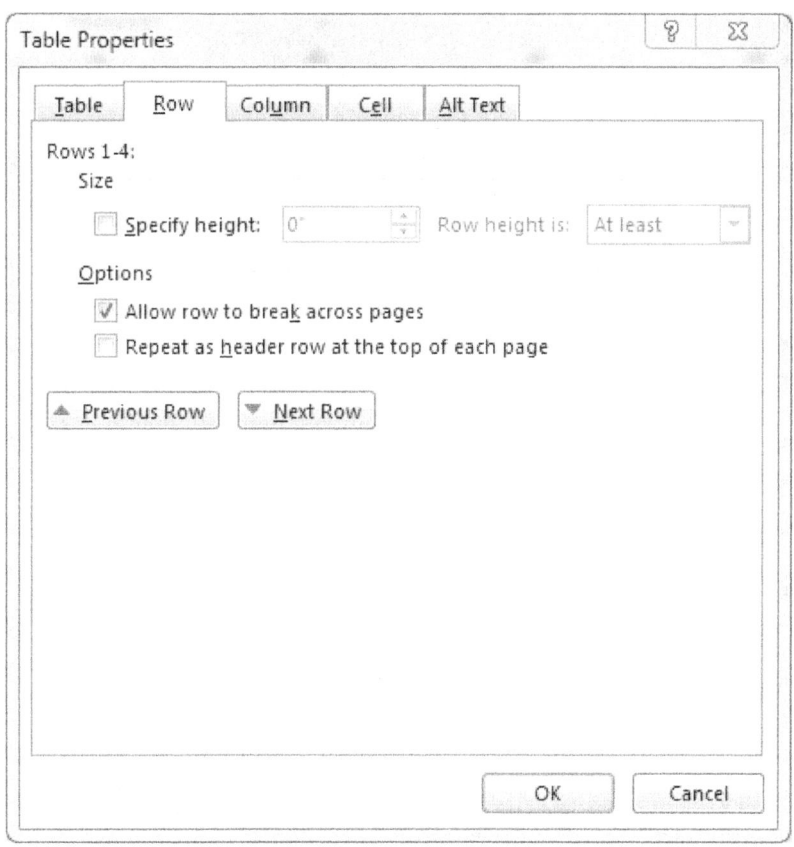

Figure 10-16. Use the Table Properties Row tab to define the selected cells' row height and the way a table behaves when it is too big to fit on a single page

<u>**Attention**</u>: Any table row height is first defined by any of its cells' Font and Paragraph properties. For better results use the same Font type and size, Line spacing = 1, and Space Before = After = 0 for all table cells.

- Specify height: this option defines the amount of vertical space added to a table cell.

MICROSOFT WORD

- Row height: use **At Least** to define a minimum cell height; use **exactly** to define a fixed cell height.

- Allow row to break across pages: uncheck this option to make each cell appear on a single document page.

- Repeat as header row at the top of each page: check this option to make a table that is big enough not to fit on a single page, automatically repeat its first row at the top of the next page (tables that fit on a page will not react to this option).

Changing Table Column Size

Column widths can be easily controlled by dragging the column right border, but to easily give to all column cells the same width, you will do better using the Paragraph.

Properties Column tab Preferred width control, which can be defined as table width percent or by specific inch value (Figure 7-17).

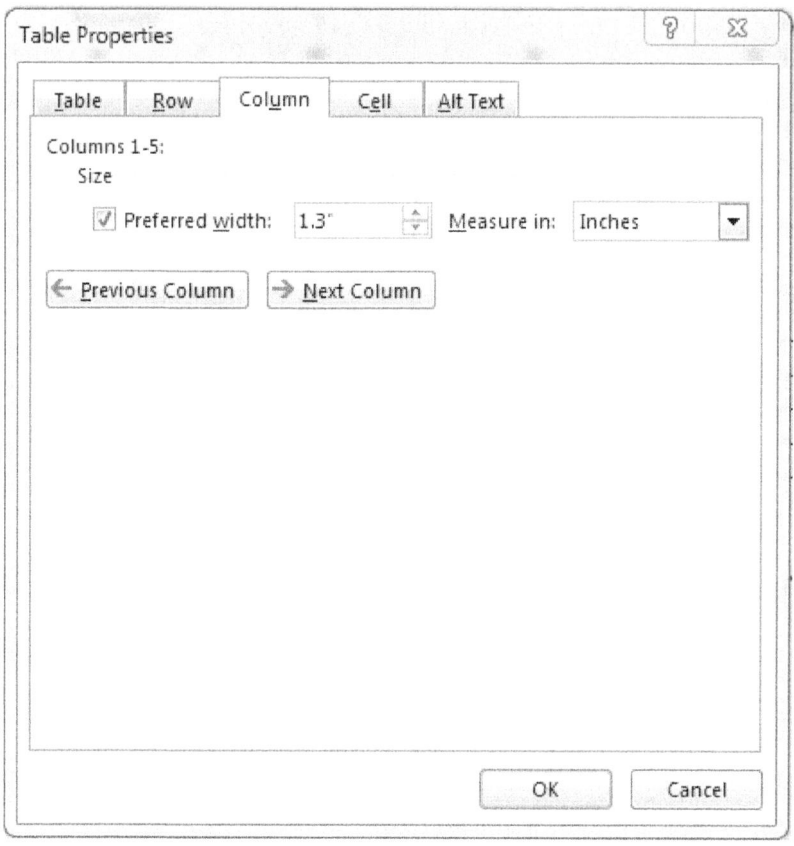

Figure 7-17. Use, the Table Properties Column, tab to apply the same column width to all selected cells, using a table width percent value or a defined column width in inches.

<u>*Attention*</u> To easily adjust a cell column width according to the column cells' content, use the same Microsoft Excel approach: double-click the column right border to make Microsoft Word adjust the column width to the widest column content.

Changing Cell Dimensions and Vertical Alignment

Use the Table Properties Cell tab to define selected cells' width and vertical alignment (since cell height may be defined by another cell of the same row or to the options set in the Table Properties Row tab).

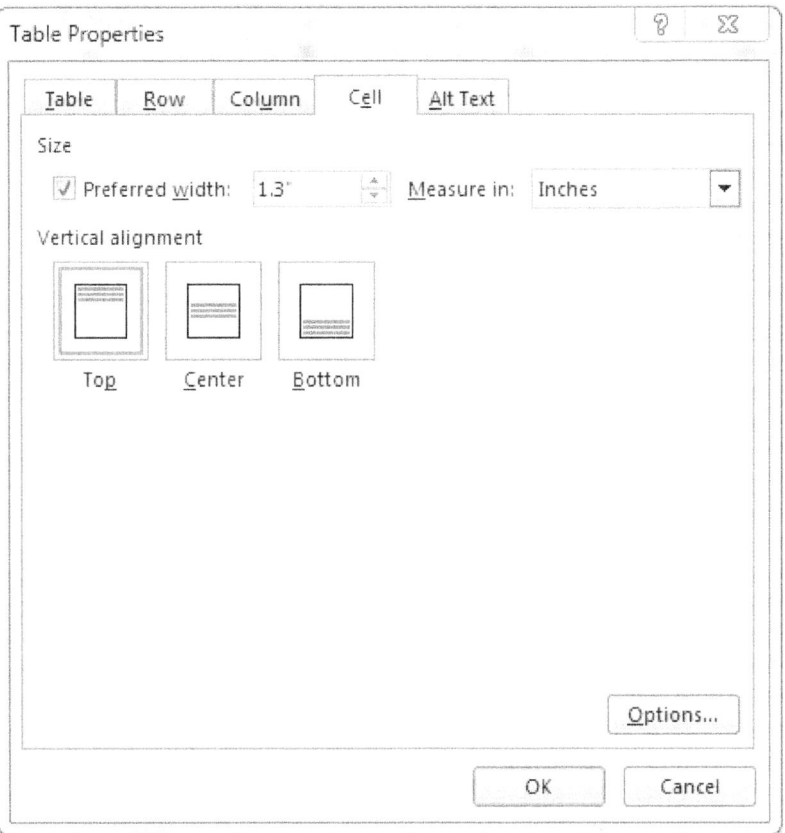

Figure 7-18. Use the Table Properties Cell tab to define selected cells' width and vertical text alignment

Attention: These options can also be set using the Table Tools Layout tab controls, as you will see in the next section.

Use the Table Properties Alt Text to insert a table text description that can be used by people with vision or cognitive impairments.

Auto-Generate Table of Content

An automatic Table of Contents keep track of page numbers and section titles for you automatically.

If you want an automatic table of contents, you need to apply the Heading 1 style to all of your chapter titles and front matter headings (e.g., "Introduction" and "Dedication"). All significant headings within your chapters should use the Heading 2 style. All subheadings should use Heading 3, and so on.

If you have used Heading styles in your document, follow these steps to generate your Table of content quickly:

- Place your cursor where you want your table of contents to be.

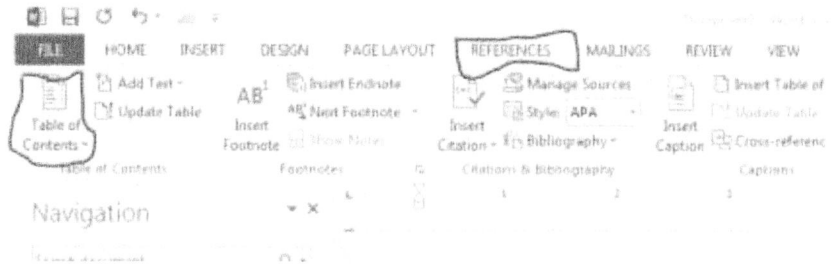

- On the References Ribbon, in the Table of Contents Group, click on the arrow next to the Table of Contents icon, and select Custom Table of Contents.

- If you want to change the style of your table of contents, click on the Modify button, select the TOC level you wish to change, then click the Modify button to do so.

- If you want to change which headings appear in your table of contents, you can change the number in the Show levels: pulldown.

- Click OK to insert your table of contents.

The table of contents is captured from the headings and page numbers in your document and does not automatically update itself as you make changes. At any time, you can update it by right-clicking on it and selecting the Update field. Notice that once the table of contents is in your document, it will turn gray if you click on it. This indicates that it is getting information from somewhere else.

CHAPTER 7

CREATING AND USING TEMPLATES

What Is a Template?

A template is a special kind of file that allows you to start a new document using a predefined set of formatting options. Templates are available for the main Microsoft Office applications

A Microsoft Word template is indeed a common .DOCX document that has the extension changed to .DOTM to allow it to be treated differently by the program (the.dotm file extension means Document Template with Macros).

By default, Microsoft Word doesn't open a template: it uses its structure to create a new, unnamed document that is a perfect copy of the original. Yes! A template is a kind of document that can make copies of itself without disturbing its own content.

Whenever you open Microsoft Word 2016, it will show you the Start Up screen (also called New window) from where you can decide which template will be used to create a new, unnamed document (Figure 8-1).

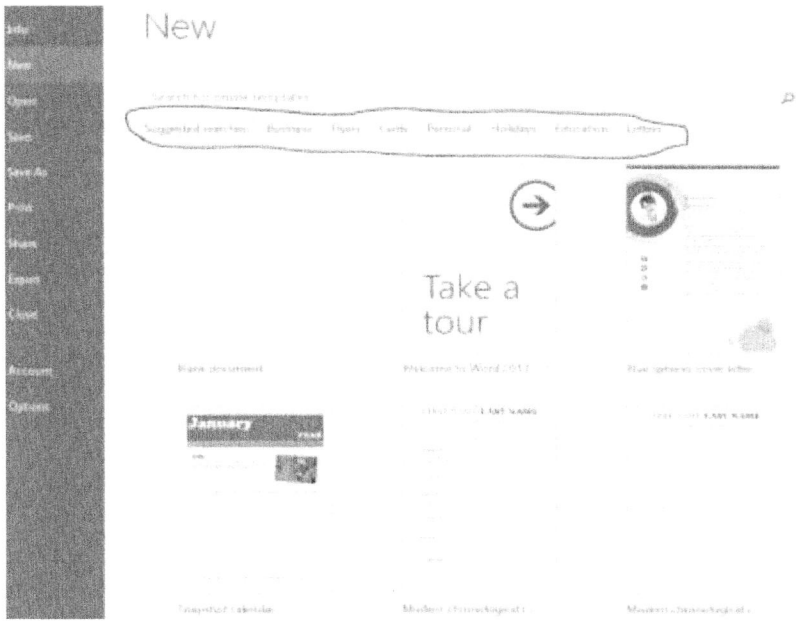

Figure 8-1. The Microsoft Word New window shows many different templates from where you can create a new document.

This window is opened by default due to the **Show the Start screen** when this application **starts option** found in the General ➤ Start up Options area of the Word Options dialog box (displayed by the File ➤ Options command, Figure 8-2).

Attention: By unchecking the Show the Start screen when this application starts option, Microsoft Word will immediately show a new, empty copy of a blank document when it is opened.

MICROSOFT WORD

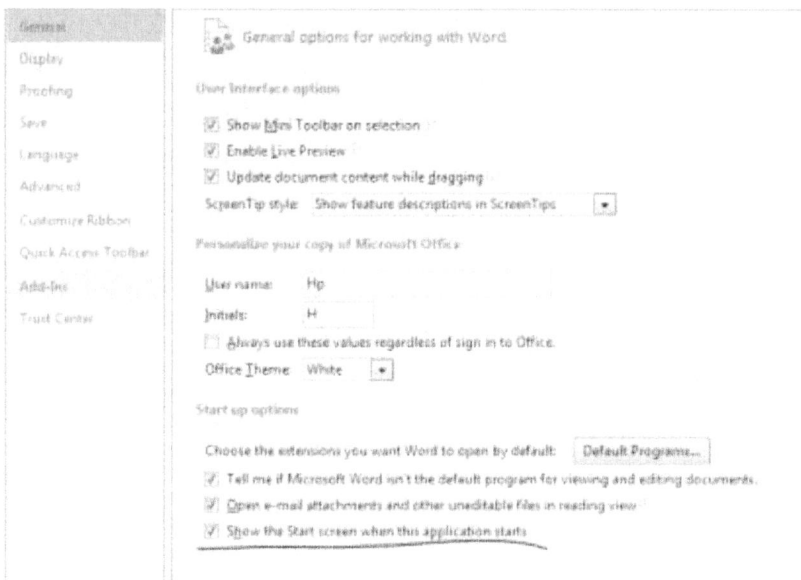

Figure 8-2. Uncheck the Show the Start screen when this application starts option, which is found in the General ➤ Start up option area of the Word Options dialog box (found using File ➤ Options).

Types of Word Templates

The New window (shown by clicking File ➤ New command) offers different types of Templates that can be used to save time when you have a need to create well-formatted special-purpose documents. It is also a source of inspiration and possibilities that you can achieve by mastering Microsoft Word features.

Try for example the "Take a Tour" template: a document that gives basic guidance about how to take the most from Microsoft Word 2016, focusing on the use of the "Tell me what you want to do" option, which is always shown in the Ribbon. Also note that although you opened the "Take a Tour" template, Microsoft Word document window shows Document1 as the document name (Figure 8-3).

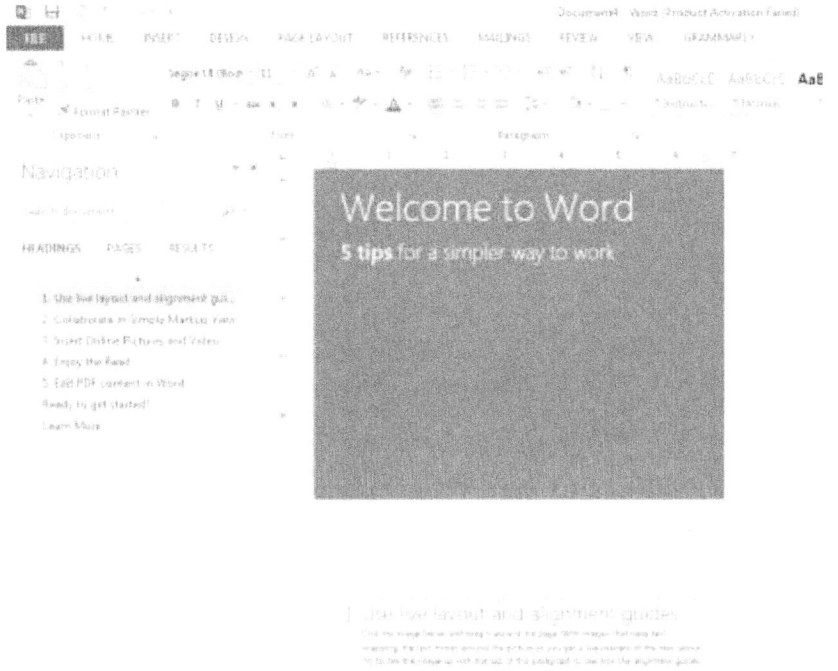

Figure 8-3. The Take, a Tour template is a simple document, prepared to guide the user to make the most of the Tell Me tool always visible above the Ribbon's right corner

There are a lot of different Microsoft Word templates to choose from, and they can be divided into three main groups:

• **Empty templates:** creates empty documents to work with (as the New Document.dotm and Single Spaced Blank.dotm shown in Figure 8-1).

- **Templates with page and style formatting:** shows special formatting pages, with graphic and design elements, from where you can type text.

- **Templates with formatting and Controls:** shows documents that have special page and style formatting options, and also have Controls that guide the user to where the information must be typed.

To understand the different types of templates, you must open and try them to see what they offer, how they were formatted, and how they work. Let's try.

Templates with Formatting and Controls

Many templates found in the New window have both page and style formatting and use Microsoft Word Controls to guide the user to insert the information in the right document places.

Since the New window changes the Templates as you select them, let's have a simple introduction about Controls using the Suggested Search: Design Sets ➤ Invoice (Green design) template (Figure 8-4).

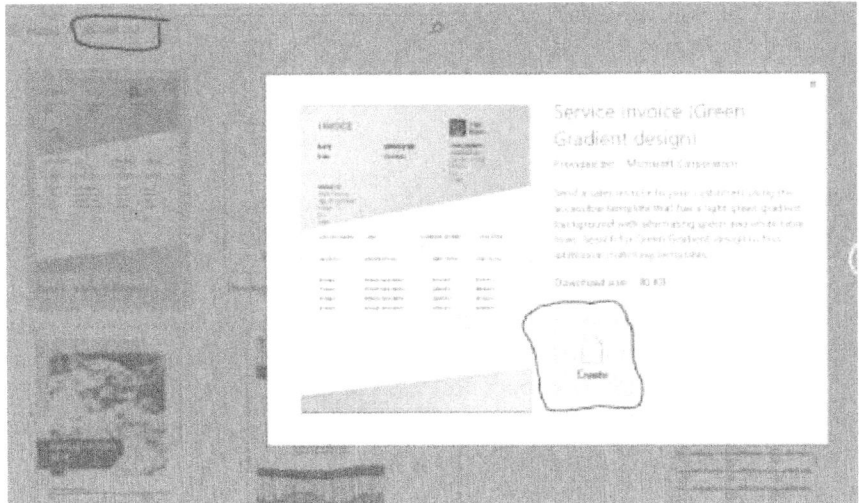

Figure 8-4. Select different Microsoft Word templates using the Suggested Search option. This figure shows the Design Sets category, with the Invoice (Green design) template appearing as the first business template.

How to personalize Microsoft template for yourself

If you frequently create a certain type of document, such as a monthly report, a sales forecast, or a presentation with a company logo, save it as a template so you can use that as your starting point instead of recreating the file from scratch each time you need it. Start with a document that you already created, a document you downloaded, or a new template you customized.

Save a template

- To save a file as a template, click File ➤ Save As.

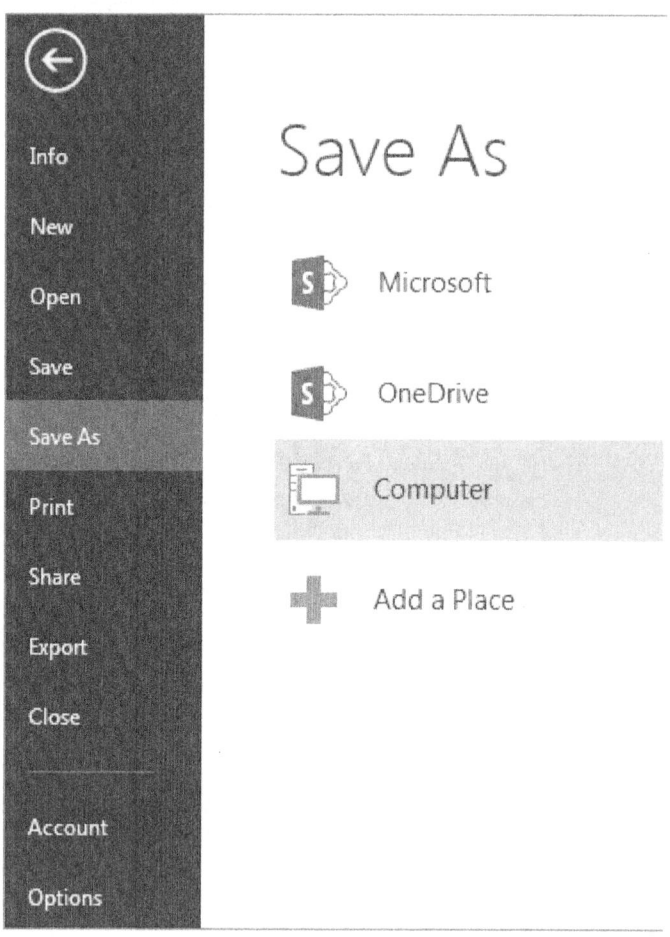

- Double-click Computer or, in Office 2016 programs, double-click This PC.
- Type a name for your template in the File name box.
- For a basic template, click the template item in the Save as type list. In Word for example, click Word Template.

MICROSOFT WORD

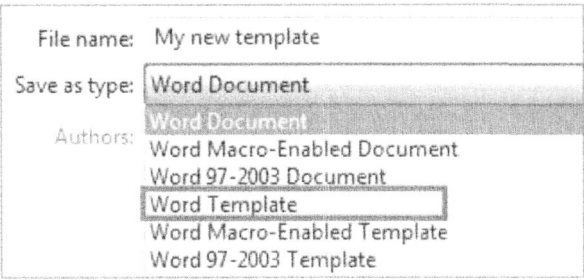

- Click Save. (**Hint**: To change where your application automatically saves your templates, click File ➤ Options ➤ Save and type the folder and path you want to use in the Default personal templates location box. Any new templates you save will be stored in that folder, and when you click File ➤ New ➤ Personal, you'll see the templates in that folder.)

Attention: If your document contains macros, click Word Macro-Enabled Template. Office automatically goes to the Custom Office Templates folder.

CHAPTER 8

COMMON MICROSOFT WORD PROBLEMS AND POSSIBLE SOLUTIONS

The last few versions of Microsoft Office have been stable, and there are hardly any issues with them. However, occasionally, you might find Microsoft Word is not responding. It just stays stuck on the screen no matter what you do.

There are many reasons Microsoft Word may, not respond. Maybe there are issues with the add-ins that you've installed? Or maybe the document you're trying to open is corrupt and causing Word to freeze-up?

Luckily, there are multiple ways to fix these issues with Word on your computer. Follow the following steps to bring your word software to work typically:

Launch Word in Safe Mode & Disable Add-Ins

One way to fix Microsoft Word when it's not responding is to use safe mode; this lets you open Word only with the essential files, and it'll help you troubleshoot any add-in issues with the app.

- Press and hold the Ctrl key on your keyboard and click the Word shortcut on your desktop.

- You'll get a prompt that asks if you want to open Word in safe mode. Click Yes to continue. (Illustrate in Figure 6-1 below)

MICROSOFT WORD

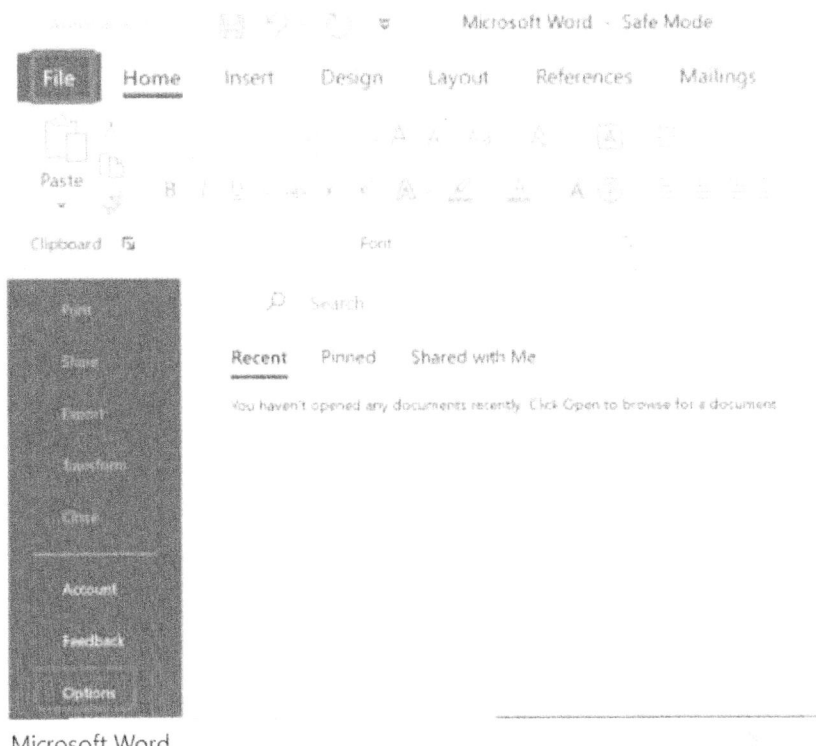

Microsoft Word

 You're holding down the CTRL key. Do you want to start Word in safe mode?

- Click the File menu at the top of your screen. (figure 6-2)

- Select Options from the left sidebar on your screen. It should be at the bottom of the list.

- On the following screen, click the Add-ins option in the left sidebar.

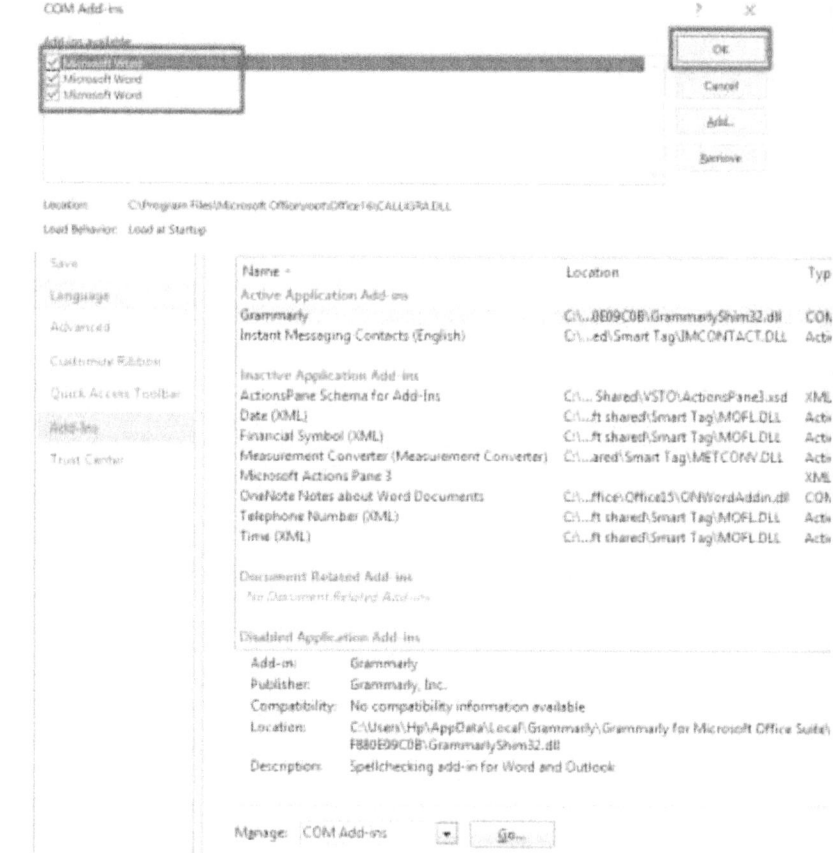

Find the Manage drop-down menu on the right-hand side pane and click **Go** next to it.

- Untick all the add-ins on your screen and click OK.

- Launch Word in normal mode, and it should open.

Problem related to editing a document

Word documents are very important in an office setting as a lot of official work and reports are done in Microsoft Word. Microsoft's Productive Suite is very easy to work in, with Microsoft Word being one of the best text editors available in the market. But what if for some reason you can't edit Word document all of a sudden? It can be especially problematic for office workers.

We understand how distressing this problem can be, which is why in this section, we have discussed several ways that can be used to diagnose and troubleshoot this problem.

Why Can't I Edit My Word Document?

There can be various reasons that can stop you from editing your Word document, let's look at the causes of this problem:

- If the trial version of the office program that you are running expires, then you can face this issue.
- The Word file may be set to open in read-only mode, which is why you are unable to edit it.
- If editing the Word document has been restricted, then this problem can occur.
- The Protected view feature that is enabled can restrict editing documents that can potentially harm your computer.
- If more than one user has the document open in a shared network, then you cannot edit the Word document.
- The file may not be a Word document (.docx) but rather converted to .doc, which is why Microsoft Word won't let you edit it.

MICROSOFT WORD

What to Do When You Can't Edit Word Document

Now that you know the various causes of this problem, it's time to troubleshoot them one by one.

Solution 1: Check Some Basic Issues

This problem can occur if you are using a trial version of the Office program and the trial period has expired. The first thing that you need to do if you are using a trial version is to check if the trial period has finished.

Next, if the document you want to edit is in any removable device, then copy it and paste it in your hard disk and then try editing it.

Then, check if the Word is asking for a password when you are trying to edit the document. If yes, then ask the owner of the document to give you the password.

Finally, check if the document you are trying to open is really a .doc file. Sometimes this problem can arise when other file formats are converted into .doc, which Microsoft Word may not allow you to edit.

Solution 2: Disable Read-Only Mode

This problem can also occur if the document has been opened in read-only mode. In this scenario, disabling the read-only mode should fix this problem.

To disable the read-only mode, follow the steps given below:

- Locate the Word document you want to edit and right-click on it.

- Click on the Properties option from the pop-up menu.

MICROSOFT WORD

- Uncheck the Read-only attribute in the General tab. See figure 6-6

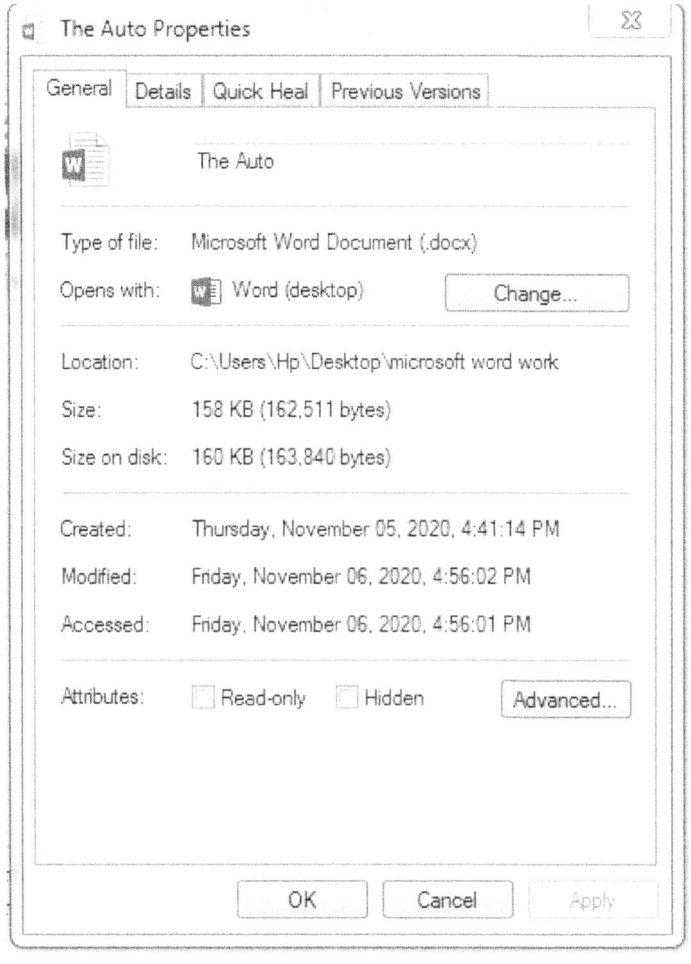

- Now, select the Security tab and see if the elements in the Group or user names section have been allowed the Full control, Modify, Read & execute, Read, Write permissions.

- If they are not allowed then, click on the Edit option below the Group or user names section and select the boxes for the options given above.

- Finally, click on Apply and OK to save all the changes.

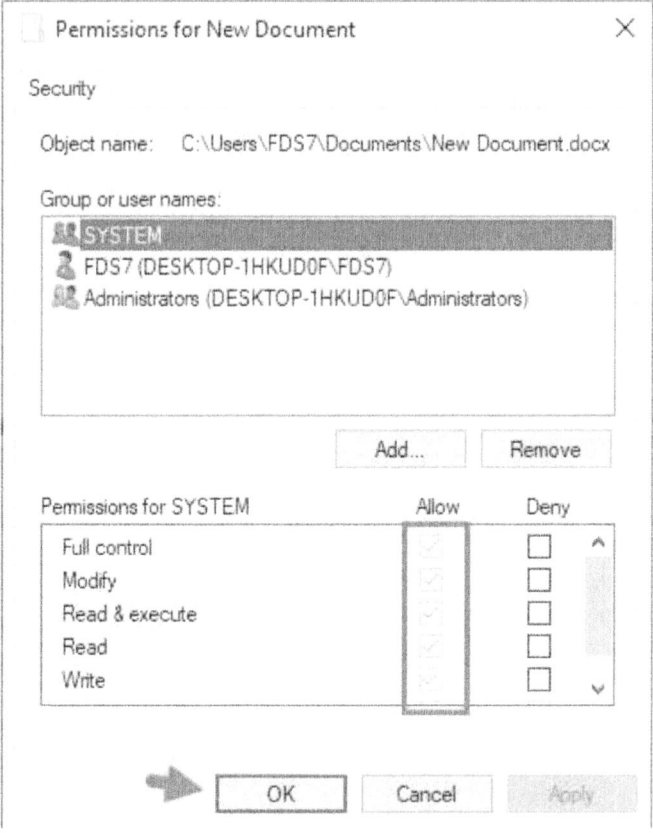

Now, check if you still can't edit Word document. This solution should fix this problem.

Solution 3: Change the Restrict Editing Settings

MICROSOFT WORD

As mentioned above, documents can be restricted to edit. If this is the case, then changing the Restrict Editing settings should fix this problem.

To change the Restrict Editing settings, follow the steps given below:

1. First, open the document in Microsoft Word and then click on the Review option.

2. Click on the Restrict Editing option. If any of the restriction boxes are selected, then uncheck them.

3. Close down the document and reopen it.

Disabling the Restrict Editing feature should solve this issue.

Solution 4: Disable The Protected View Feature

The Protected View feature in Microsoft Word basically opens the potentially malicious documents in a restricted mode. Thus, this security feature can stop you from editing the Word document if it considers the document as malicious or a threat to your computer.

To disable Protected view, follow the steps given below:

1. Open the document in the Microsoft Word and click on the File option.

2. Scroll down and click on the Options. It will open the Word options panel on your computer.

3. Now, click on the Trust Centre option and then click on the Trust Centre Settings.

4. Click on the Protected View option.

MICROSOFT WORD

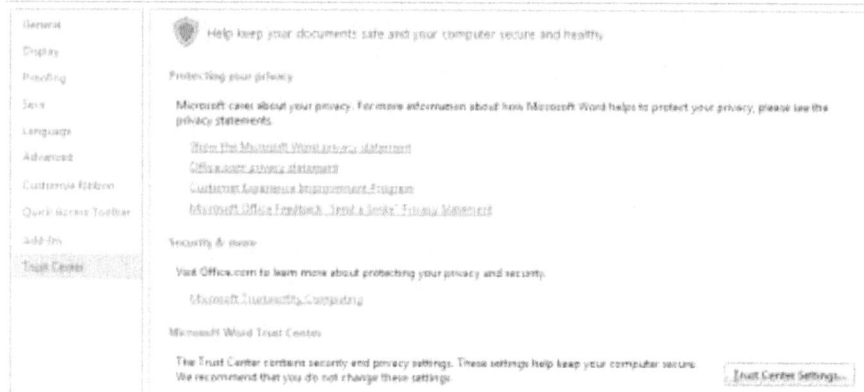

5. Now, uncheck all the options related to Protected View and then click on OK.

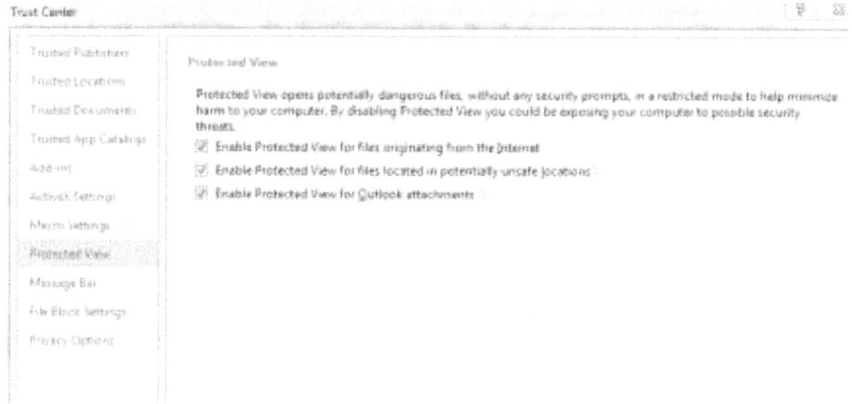

Figure 6-8 Disable protected view

Close the document and then reopen it. Check if you are able to edit it or not. If you still cannot edit Word document, then try the next solution.

MICROSOFT WORD

TEN FUNCTION KEY

Shortcuts

A long time ago, it was popular to use something called a keyboard template. You'd place this cardboard cutout over the top of the computer's keyboard.

Its legend described commands associated with the function keys. Back in those days, the keyboard was the primary input device, and people preferred using function keys over using the mouse.

Thanks to the Ribbon interface, Word is now a lot easier to use than in the old keyboard days. Still, those keyboard shortcuts linger. Some of them are pretty handy, though not memorable. I've listed them all here in this chapter.

And yes, I confess that because 12 function keys adorn the top of your PC's keyboard, this chapter features 12 function key shortcuts, not as the ten advertised.

The function key commands here are listed as they are mapped within Word. Other programs installed on your computer may hijack certain key combinations.

Also, some laptop computers may require you to press the Fn key in combination with the function keys to fully access their features.

F1

- Unmodified Displày is the online Help for Word 2016. You can search for help, browse categories, and be otherwise baffled by the information displayed.

- Shift Display (or hide) reveals formatting pane.

- The Ctrl, Show hides the Ribbon.

MICROSOFT WORD

- Alt is to go to the next field.
- Shift+Ctrl maximizes the document window to fill the screen and hide the Ribbon.
- Shift+Alt, Go to the previous field in the document.
- Ctrl+Alt, Display the System Information window.

F2

- Unmodified Move command. Select text and press F2. Click to position the insertion pointer, and then press the Enter key to cut and paste the selected block.
- Shift Copy to command. Select text and press Shift+F2. Move the insertion pointer and press Enter to copy the selected text.
- Ctrl activates the Print Preview screen; the same as pressing.
- Ctrl+P.
- Shift+Alt is the Save command; same as Ctrl+S.
- Ctrl+Alt brings up the Open dialog box.

F3

- Unmodified Insert building block. Type the first part of the building block text, and then press F3.
- Shift Change Case command. Press Shift+F3 to cycle between lowercase, uppercase, and Sentence Case formats.
- Ctrl Cut selected text and store it in the Spike. The Spike can contain a collection of cut items, similar to the Clipboard; however, spiked items are not stored in the Clipboard.

MICROSOFT WORD

- Alt Create a new Building Block entry. After you press Alt+F3, the Create New Building Block dialog box appears.

- Shift+Ctrl Paste the contents of the spike. All spiked items (cut with Ctrl+F3) are inserted into the document. This is not the same command as Ctrl+V.

F4

- Unmodified Repeat command; the same as Ctrl+Y or Redo.

- Shift Repeat last browsed object, such as Repeat Last Find or repeat the last Go To command, such as Go to Page.

- Ctrl Close the window; the same as the Ctrl+W command.

- Alt quit the program. The Alt+F4 keyboard shortcut is the standard Windows command to close any window or program.

- Shift+Alt Close the window; the same as Ctrl+W and Ctrl+F4.

F5

- Unmodified activates the Go to dialog box, or the Find and Replace dialog box with the Go to tab forward.

- Shift Move the insertion pointer to the last edit in the document.

- This command can be repeated four times to cycle through various locations.

- Ctrl Restore document window.

- Alt Restore program window.

- Shift+Ctrl Display the Bookmark dialog box.

MICROSOFT WORD

F6

- Unmodified Cycle to the next open frame or pane.
- Shift Cycle to the previous open frame or pane.
- Ctrl Cycle to the next document window.
- Alt will cycle to the next document window; the same as Ctrl+F6.
- Shift+Ctrl Cycle to the previous document window.
- Shift+Alt Cycle to the previous document window; the same as Shift+Ctrl+F6.

F7

- Unmodified Proof the document.
- Shift Open the Thesaurus pane for the current word.
- Alt Move the insertion pointer to the next misspelled word.
- Shift+Ctrl Update Source command. This command applies to the IncludeText field and directs Word to update the contents based on the source document.
- Shift+Alt Open the Translation pane for the current word.
- Ctrl+Alt Summon the Korean-language spell checker. (I believe that this assignment is a bug.)

F8

- Unmodified Activate extended selection mode. Use the cursor keys to extend the selection; type a character to extend the selection; press F8 again to select a larger document chunk.

MICROSOFT WORD

- Shift Shrink the extended selection—Press Shift+F8 to undo the last F8 key press.

- Alt Display the Macros dialog box.

- Shift+Ctrl Enter block selection mode. In this mode, you select a rectangular chunk of text. Use the cursor keys or mouse to highlight a rectangle of text in the document. You can work with the block selection just as you can with any chunk of selected text.

F9

- Unmodified Update the current field: Click in a field and press the F9 key.

- The Ctrl+Shift+U key does the same thing.

- Ctrl Insert an empty field, a pair of curly brackets with nothing between them.

- Alt will toggle field codes for all fields in the document.

- Shift+Ctrl Convert the current field into plain text.

- Shift+Alt simulate a user clicking on a field for programming macros.

- Unmodified Display Ribbon accelerator-key shortcuts.

- Shift Nonfunctioning shortcut menu command.

- Ctrl Maximize the document window.

- Alt Show or hide the Selection pane.

- Shift+Ctrl Assigned to the WW2_RulerMode command, which no one knows anything about.

- Shift+Alt Displays the smart tag menu.

MICROSOFT WORD

F11

- Unmodified Go to the next field in the document.
- Shift Go to the previous field in the document.
- Ctrl Lock the field.
- Alt Display the Visual Basic Editor.
- Shift+Ctrl unlock the field.

F12

- Unmodified will ummon the **Save As dialog** box. This command works whether or not the document has been saved.
- Shift will bring up the Save As screen if the document hasn't already been saved.
- Ctrl activates the Open dialog box.
- Shift+Ctrl enables the Print screen; the same as Ctrl+P.
- Shift+Alt activates the button on a selected content control.

Printed in Great Britain
by Amazon